BUSINESS
with INTEGRITY

BUSINESS
with INTEGRITY

EXECUTIVES *and* EDUCATORS
SHARE EXPERIENCES *and* INSIGHTS

EDITED BY
J. Melody Murdock and Joseph D. Ogden

BRIGHAM YOUNG UNIVERSITY PRESS
PROVO, UTAH

Marriott School of Management
Brigham Young University
490 Tanner Building
Provo, Utah 84602

Brigham Young University Press
Provo, Utah 84602

ISBN: 0-8425-2628-5

GRAPHIC DESIGN: Jon G. Woidka
COVER ILLUSTRATION: Jon C. Lund

Printed in the United States of America.

Printed on acid-free paper.

8/05 | 05-124 | 7,500 | 19086

TO MARRIOTT SCHOOL STUDENTS,
GRADUATES, FACULTY, AND THOSE WHO SHARE
A COMMITMENT TO INTEGRITY IN BUSINESS

CONTENTS

FOREWORD

S ome time ago I was asked to consult for a bank that was having a problem with employee morale. "I don't know what's wrong," bemoaned their young president. Bright and charismatic, he'd risen through the ranks only to see his institution faltering. Productivity and profits were down. He blamed his employees. "No matter what incentives I provide," he said, "they won't shake off this gloom and doom." He was right. The atmosphere seemed poisoned with suspicion and lack of trust. For months I ran workshops, but nothing helped. I was stumped.

"How can anyone trust what's happening here?" was a typical employee refrain. But no one would tell me the source of the distrust.

Finally, in more casual conversations with employees, the truth emerged. The boss, who was married, was having an affair with an employee. And everyone knew it. It was obvious now that the company's poor performance was caused by his conduct. But the greatest damage this man was doing was to himself. He was thinking only of his own gratification, disregarding long-term consequences. Moreover, he had violated a sacred trust with his wife. In a word, his failing was one of character. I'm convinced 90 percent of all leadership failures are failures of character, not ability.

What became of the bank president? When I confided to him what I knew of his affair and the effect it was having on his staff, he ran his fingers through his hair. "I don't know where to begin," he said.

"Is it over?" I asked.

He looked me squarely in the eye. "Yes. Absolutely."

"Then begin by talking with your wife," I answered.

He told his wife, who forgave him. Then he called a meeting of his staff and addressed their morale problem. "I have found the cause of the problem," he said. "It is me. I am asking you to give me another chance."

It took time, but eventually employee morale—a sense of openness, optimism, and trust—improved. In the end, however, the executive was doing himself the greatest favor. He was finding his own path to integrity.

PRIMARY AND SECONDARY GREATNESS

Someone wrote, "When man found the mirror he began to lose his soul." The point is he became more concerned with his image than with himself.

Positive personality traits, while often essential for success, constitute secondary greatness. To focus on personality before character is to try to grow the leaves without the roots.

If we consistently use personality techniques and skills to enhance our social interactions, we may truncate the vital character base. We simply can't have the fruits without the roots. Private victory precedes public victory.

Many people with secondary greatness—that is, social status, position, fame, wealth, or talent—lack primary greatness or goodness of character. And this void is evident in every long-term relationship they have, whether it is with a business associate, a spouse, a friend, or a teenage child. It is a character of integrity that communicates most eloquently. As Ralph Waldo Emerson once put it, "What you are shouts so loud in my ears I cannot hear what you say."

Of course, people may have character strength but lack key communication skills or other needed competencies—and that undoubtedly affects the quality of their relationships as well. But in the last analysis, what we are communicates far more eloquently than anything we say or do. Theodore Roosevelt said, "Character, in the long run, is the decisive factor in the life of an individual and of nations alike."

As you read through the splendid and varied contributions of the executives and educators in this book, you will come to sense that they are people with both primary and secondary greatness—that is, they are people of primary greatness, which is based on character and contribution, and also of secondary greatness based on their outward successes and their prominence. Although each of them would defer from my categorizing them as models of both primary and secondary greatness, nevertheless, I personally believe it to be so. Greatness is defined by the Savior as the servant: ". . . the same is appointed to be the greatest, notwithstanding he is the least and the servant of all."[1] You can feel the sense of stewardship and of servant leadership in the spirit of these writers. I believe each would give credit to God as the source of the principles that have enabled their contributions in life.

The founder of the modern servant leadership movement, Robert Greenleaf, said, "A new moral principle is emerging which holds that the only authority deserving one's allegiance is that which is freely and knowingly granted by the led to the leader in response to, and in proportion to, the clearly evident servant stature of the leader. Those who choose to follow this principle will not casually accept the authority of existing institutions. Rather, they will freely respond only to individuals who are chosen as leaders because they are proven and trusted as servants. To the extent that this principle prevails in the future, the only truly viable institutions will be those that are predominantly servant-led."

THE PARENTS AND CHILDREN OF INTEGRITY

Let me suggest a way of thinking about integrity that may be a useful framework as you read the contributions in this book, because even though they do not always use the words I'm using, I think you will sense the same meaning from their words. The following figure is a two-generation diagram depicting both the parents and children of integrity, with the opposite also depicted just below the virtue identified, i.e. the opposite of integrity is duplicity and hypocrisy.

We might say that humility is the mother of all virtues, including integrity, and that courage is the father. When people follow true principles courageously in difficult and tempting circumstances, they cultivate integrity and personal security. Their sense of worth does not come from being compared with others, and therefore, they develop an abundance mentality—seeing

PRINCIPLE-CENTERED LIVING: TWO GENERATIONS

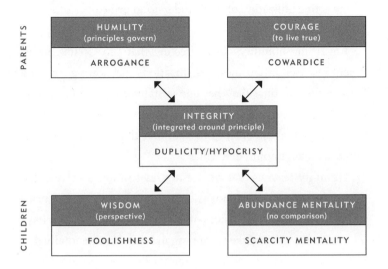

life as a cornucopia of resources and opportunities. The great Christian apologist, C. S. Lewis, said, "Pride gets no pleasure out of having something, only out of having more of it than the next man. . . . It is the comparison that makes you proud: the pleasure of being above the rest. Once the element of competition has gone, pride has gone."

Another child of humility and courage is wisdom, because sound understanding and good judgment as well as an eternal perspective are the fruits of life with integrity.

When you fill purpose and activity with principles, you get wisdom. As Alfred North Whitehead once said, "In a sense, knowledge shrinks as wisdom grows, for details are swallowed up in principles. The details for knowledge, which are important, will be picked up ad hoc in each avocation of life, but the habit of the active utilization of well-understood principles is the final possession of wisdom."

Regarding humility, it's interesting that Jim Collins, in his recent research on business organizations that were good for a long period of time then became sustainably great for a long period of time, wrote there was one quality that every top executive running these businesses had, and that is humility combined with an indomitable will.

Humility teaches that we are not laws unto ourselves, that principles govern. Behavior is driven by our values, but principles drive the consequences of our behavior. You could have a social value system like cramming in school but be totally disconnected from principles. In other words, you can get a degree but you won't get an education. And when you're in business attempting to build high trust among your stakeholders, again, there is no way to cram it through. There's no quick fix. The value systems in that business must be based upon principles. Here is a brief description of the difference between values and principles.

VALUES	PRINCIPLES
Social Norms	Natural Laws
Personal	Impersonal
Emotional	Factual
Subjective	Objective
Arguable	Self-Evident

When we cultivate a spiritually educated conscience, our conscience becomes a repository of principles and is the opposite of ego. For a moment, let's drill down on conscience and ego.

Conscience is the still, small voice within. It is quiet. It is peaceful. Ego is tyrannical, despotic, and dictatorial.

Ego focuses on one's own survival, pleasure, and enhancement to the exclusion of others and is selfishly ambitious. It sees relationships in terms of threat or no threat like little children who classify all people as "nice" or "mean." Conscience, on the other hand, both democratizes and elevates ego to a larger sense of the group, the whole, the community, the greater good. It sees life in terms of service and contribution, in terms of others' security and fulfillment.

Ego works in the face of genuine crisis but has no discernment in deciding how severe a crises or threat is. Conscience is filled with discernment and senses the degree of threat. It has a large repertoire of responses. It has the patience and wisdom to decide what to do when. Conscience sees life on a continuum. It's capable of complex adaptation.

Ego can't sleep. It micromanages. It disempowers. It reduces one's capacity. It excels in control. Conscience deeply reveres people and sees their potential for self-control. Conscience empowers. It reflects the worth and value of all people and affirms their power and freedom to choose. Then natural self-control emerges, imposed neither from above nor from the outside.

Ego is threatened by negative feedback and punishes the messenger. It interprets all data in terms of self-preservation. It constantly censors information. It denies much of reality.

Conscience values feedback and attempts to discern whatever truth it contains. It isn't afraid of information and can accurately interpret what's going on. It has no need to censor information and is open to an awareness of reality from every direction.

Conscience teaches us that ends and means are inseparable, that ends actually preexist in the means. Immanuel Kant taught that the means used to accomplish the ends are as important as those ends. Machiavelli taught the opposite, that the ends justify the means.

Consider the seven things that Gandhi taught will destroy us. Each represents an end being accomplished through an unprincipled or unworthy means:

- Wealth without work
- Pleasure without conscience
- Knowledge without character
- Commerce without morality
- Science without humanity
- Worship without sacrifice
- Politics without principle

Isn't it interesting how each one of these admirable ends can be falsely attained? But if you reach an admirable end through the wrong means, the ends ultimately turn to dust in your hands.

In your business dealings, you come to know those who are honest with you and who keep their promises and commitments. You also know exactly who is duplicitous, deceitful, and dishonest. Even when you reach a legal agreement with people who are dishonest, do you really trust they'll keep their word?

In this book you'll discover that the test of whether people live with integrity comes in moments of pressure, stress, temptation, and exhaustion. As Vince Lombardi put it, "Fatigue makes cowards of us all." So that's when we have to exercise great courage. President Harold B. Lee taught that "courage is the quality of every virtue acting at its highest testing point." It comes from having a larger sense of what is truly important, a burning conviction regarding your purpose or a cause and how those ends preexist in the means.

TRUST

The ultimate fruit of integrity or trustworthiness is trust. Trust is the glue of life. Think about it at the most elementary level—getting up in the morning, having breakfast, saying goodbye to your loved ones, and driving your car to work. Every activity is based on the trust you have in those who provide power to your home, the competence of the school bus driver, and the honesty of the civil engineers, construction people, and automobile manufacturers in providing functional, safe roads and cars. Often we're like fish who discover water last—unaware of the element that we are immersed in. Just as trust comes from trustworthiness, trustworthiness comes from character and competence.

The twenty-first century opened with a barrage of corporate accounting scandals that brought the importance of trust and personal character back to the forefront. Leadership in this century will be defined by personal integrity and character. My son, Stephen M. R. Covey, together with his firm, CoveyLink Worldwide, has been making an in-depth study of the high cost of low trust. He shared the following findings with me. First, only 36 percent of employees believe top managers act with honesty and integrity.[2] Second, only 37 percent of employees believe the information they receive from management.[3] Third, only 34 percent of Americans believe other people can be trusted.[4] Fourth, only 51 percent of workers say their companies are open and honest.[5] And fifth, only 6 percent of employees who believe their senior management is unethical are inclined to stay with their companies (vs. 40 percent who are inclined to stay because they believe their senior management is ethical).[6]

FranklinCovey surveyed more than fifty-four thousand people and asked them to identify the essential qualities of a leader; integrity was, by far, the number one response.

Additionally, see the following chart, which estimates the high cost of low integrity in business today.

ANNUAL COST IN THE U.S.

Employee fraud	$400 billion*
Time theft	$230 billion*
Industrial espionage	$200 billion*
Counterfeiting	$200 billion*
Employee dishonesty	$120 billion*
Identity theft	$50 billion**

*Source: Fast Company, *December 2004*
**Source: www.fightidentitytheft.com

MARRIOTT SCHOOL OF MANAGEMENT STEWARDSHIP

The Marriott School's mission is to attract, develop, and place men and women of faith, character, and professional ability who will become outstanding leaders capable of dealing with change in a global environment.

Notice the sequence of what is focused upon—first, faith; second, character; and third, professional ability. Henry David Thoreau taught, "For every thousand hacking at the leaves of evil, there is one striking at the root." I believe that the root of a great deal of the lack of integrity comes from personal insecurity, and that dishonesty, greed, and unethical behavior is an effort to compensate for that. The first principle of the gospel is faith in the Lord Jesus Christ. It is also the main source of personal security, together with living true to that faith—what we are calling integrity or character. Then competence, or professional ability, comes into play. This is why in my judgment BYU has a unique stewardship to be a powerful leavening influence throughout all businesses and organizations, to be an educational light on the hill. Values and ethics are not a compartment in the curriculum; they are integrated throughout every department, discipline, and field of study. More and more recognition is coming to BYU for this reason. That's why the Marriott School is ranked by *The Wall Street Journal* as one of the top schools from which to hire ethical graduates.

Another reason this book was compiled is to serve as a reminder to students, faculty, and alumni of this very sacred stewardship and of the high ideals the Marriott School seeks to espouse. In a fairly recent excerpt from *The Wall Street Journal*'s guide to business schools, 22 September 2004, the recruiters' top picks state, "Among the twenty attributes in *The Wall Street Journal* survey, ethics and integrity ranked third on the priority list, behind only communication and interpersonal skills, and the ability to work well in teams." When you think about it, communication and interpersonal skills and teamwork are also based on ethics and integrity. The guide goes on to say, "Although many MBA programs have been focused more on ethics, some recruiters believe schools still aren't emphasizing integrity enough and aren't taking enough responsibility for having turned out so many 'win at any cost' graduates."

Willis Harmon, the cofounder of the World Business Academy, expressed his conviction about the institution of business itself in these words: "Business has become the most powerful institution on the planet. The dominant institution in any society needs to take responsibility for the whole. But business has not had such a tradition. This is a new role, not well understood or accepted. Built on the concept of capitalism and free enterprise from the beginning was the assumption that the actions of many units of individual enterprise, responding to market forces and guided by the 'invisible hand' of Adam Smith, would somehow add up to desirable outcomes. But in the last decade of the twentieth century, it has become clear that the 'invisible hand' is faltering. It depended on over-arching meanings and values that are no longer present. So business has to adopt a tradition it has never had throughout the entire history of capitalism: to share the responsibility of the whole. Every decision that is made, every action that is taken, must be viewed in light of that responsibility."

The essence of this kind of stewardship and leadership is moral authority, not formal authority, and those who do have formal authority will find that it will only be sustainable as they stay principle centered, ethical, and full of integrity. It is wise counsel to avoid the temptations to exercise unrighteous dominion and instead use the power of righteous influence, "by persuasion, by long-suffering, by gentleness and meekness, and by love unfeigned; by kindness, and pure knowledge, which shall greatly enlarge the soul without hypocrisy, and without guile."[7]

As you read this compilation of outstanding speeches on integrity, I encourage an earnest, prayerful effort to internalize and apply the practical messages and the underlying spiritual roots.

~Stephen R. Covey
Organizational strategy expert and
international best-selling author

ENDNOTES

1   Doctrine and Covenants 50:26.

2   Harris Interactive Study, 2004.

3   Watson Wyatt Work USA Study, 2002.

4   David Halpern, 2003.

5   Towers Perrin Study, 2004.

6   Business for Social Responsibility Survey by Walker Information, 2001.

7   Doctrine and Covenants 121:41–42.

PREFACE

his book has its genesis in two occurrences: the dramatic fallout from the accounting scandals that ushered in this century and a trip to Hong Kong by two Marriott School administrators.

First, the economic damage caused by the collapse of companies such as WorldCom and Enron not only eviscerated thousands of employees' pensions and investment dreams; it launched a new era of business. Trust has never been more questioned or valued. Companies more than ever are concerned about character. Following the scandals, many changed their recruiting procedures to seek out business school graduates with high ethical standards. Schools around the globe added new courses and modified curriculums to elevate ethics. Although the Marriott School at BYU has always valued the development of high moral standards, these scandals focused attention on the school's unique mission to prepare leaders—men and women of faith, character, and professional ability—who will positively impact the world.

Second, Dean Ned Hill and Assistant Dean Joseph Ogden met with members of the Hong Kong Chapter of the BYU Management Society in November 2003. During a lunch meeting a Marriott School graduate, now the general manager of a large exporting company, recounted a story. The graduate explained how her company's efforts to expand wholesale operations into

Australia had been thwarted by fraud. Distressed by the dishonest behavior of his contacts, the company's owner turned to the BYU graduate and said, "I trust you. Can you help us find an honest person we can work with in Australia?" She contacted someone she knew who shared her values and standards. The company took off in Australia.

This story demonstrates the power of personal experience and role models. In an effort to share uplifting stories like this, the school's external relations office and the National Advisory Council's public relations committee compiled this book of fifteen of the most compelling lectures and speeches delivered at BYU about integrity and character. The stories and examples shared in the pages that follow are evidence that having integrity and succeeding in business are not contradictory but, in fact, complementary.

ACKNOWLEDGMENTS

Thanks are due to the members of the Marriott School National Advisory Council Public Relations Committee—specifically Steve Lundgren, Jeff Smith, John Taylor, Cathy Chamberlain, and Lane Beattie—who read dozens of speeches and helped make the selections found in this book. They were also instrumental in refining the book's focus and content.

Thanks are also due to the members of the *Business with Integrity* editorial committee: Byron Bronk, Norman Darais, Doug Maxwell, Melody Murdock, Joseph Ogden, and Jon Woidka. This group managed the permissions, editing, design, and publishing.

Additional thanks to Sheri Dew and Debbie Simmons at Deseret Book for their publishing and marketing expertise; Lee Perry and Robert Gardner for their advice; and Emily Smurthwaite and Natalie Miles for their help with editing and indexing.

Finally, we acknowledge the generous contributions of the authors.

BUSINESS
with INTEGRITY

NAVIGATING IN A TOPSY-TURVY WORLD: FOUR STRATEGIES TO MAINTAIN MOMENTUM

by W. STEVE ALBRECHT

"When we judge ourselves by our intentions,
we rationalize our shortcomings and give ourselves
more credit than we deserve."

Together with you, I watched with horror and sadness the tragic events of 11 September 2001. My heart goes out to all the victims, their families, and their loved ones. I have also watched the tremendous negative effect those events have had on the economy. Nearly the entire world is now in a recession. The terrorist acts, combined with technological advances and globalization, are causing the world to change faster than ever before.

Today's business environment is topsy-turvy with declining ethics, decreasing job security, and increased social and business problems. Yet, there are more opportunities than ever before. To help Marriott School graduates navigate and maintain momentum in this fast-paced business world, I offer four strategies: 1) have a sense of value and purpose beyond work, 2) keep nimble and maximize options, 3) add value every day, and 4) avoid self-defeating behaviors.

STRATEGY 1: HAVE A SENSE OF VALUE AND PURPOSE BEYOND WORK
Fortunately, with our knowledge of the gospel, it is easy to have a purpose beyond our jobs. We know that we are much more than workers—we are children of God and have the potential to become like Him. We also know that the family unit is the only enduring organization, and that building a strong family is far more important than anything we will ever do at work.

A number of years ago, I had a memorable conversation with a student of mine in the MBA program at Stanford. I asked him what he was going to do when he graduated. He answered that he was going home to take over the family business—the Almond Roca Company. Today, he is president and CEO of that company. I thought at the time how lucky this young man was—his father handed him a very profitable company. But then I realized that we are all blessed beyond measure because our Father in Heaven has so much to offer each of us as His children. In Doctrine and Covenants, we read, "And he that receiveth my Father receiveth my Father's kingdom; therefore all that my Father hath shall be given unto him."[1] Let us never forget what is really important in life.

I look back on my life, and while I have had a wonderful career and hope to have many more productive years, what has given me the most joy has been coaching my son's baseball games, attending my daughter's clogging competitions, fishing, being in the mountains, and spending time with family. Prioritizing these types of experiences becomes increasingly difficult because they usually don't have deadlines or timetables like our job responsibilities and other commitments.

We have to be proactive to make family and the gospel top priorities—anchoring our lives on things of eternal worth. Our greatest happiness comes from being with our families, performing service, and living gospel principles. We should never let anything—work, personal hobbies, friends, or even church—come before family.

STRATEGY 2: KEEP NIMBLE AND MAXIMIZE OPTIONS

One of the reasons Heavenly Father sent us to this earth was to see if we could make good choices. A prerequisite to making good choices is having freedom. In fact, it is the ability to make choices that gives us freedom. In this fast-changing world, we must do everything possible to maximize our options and choices—hence, freedom. Although we live in a free country and have few, if any, externally imposed constraints, many of us lose or limit our freedom by choices we make. When the future is uncertain, as it is today, it pays to maintain a broad range of options. Option theory rewards flexibility.

The following recommendations will help maximize options—keeping you nimble and ready to act.

Build a good reputation. People with tarnished reputations lose options. This loss of options can affect both family and professional life. In Arthur Miller's play, "All My Sons," a son sees his father cheating in the business world. When confronted, his dad responds, "Son, everybody does it. You have to cheat to be successful." The son replies, "I know dad, but I thought you were better than everyone else." This father lost options with his son.

Losing professional options can be just as damaging. I know a woman who devoted thirty-seven years to a corporation—thirty-four of which were honest. During her last three years, she started embezzling and eventually stole $686,000. When caught, the company took her home, cars, retirement account, and most of her other assets—recovering about $400,000. She lost her reputation for honesty and the respect of her friends and was sentenced to serve one year in a federal prison. She is now out of prison but must make monthly restitution payments of $333 to the company and $540 to the IRS. If she misses one payment, she violates her parole and goes back to jail. She lost options.

Both these examples teach us that we will have many more options in the future if we build a good reputation and name. As it says in Ecclesiastes, "A good name is better than precious ointment."[2]

Become a lifelong learner. With the fast-paced changes we are experiencing, the knowledge you learned at BYU probably won't be relevant very long. You must get as much education and learning as you can throughout your life. Brigham Young said, "We might ask, when shall we cease to learn? I will give you my opinion about it; never, never . . . . We shall never cease to learn, unless we apostatize from the religion of Jesus Christ."[3]

Maintain good health. When you lose your health or become addicted to harmful substances or habits, you lose freedom. Doctrine and Covenants section 89 contains a promise about these health options if we live according to the Word of Wisdom. "And all saints who remember to keep and do these sayings [meaning maintaining good health and following the word of wisdom], walking in obedience to the commandments, shall receive health in their navel and marrow to their bones. And shall find wisdom and great treasures of knowledge, even hidden treasures; And shall run and not be weary, and shall walk and not faint."[4]

Preserve financial freedom. We live in a world in which everyone borrows. For every net saver in the United States, there are approximately nineteen net borrowers. Almost every day in the mail we get solicitations from companies wanting to extend us credit. They use glowing terms and phrases about financial freedom, but what they really want is for us to enter into financial bondage with them.

When we take debt upon ourselves, we lose freedom and options and the ability to act quickly and independently because someone else tells us how to spend our money. If we are encumbered with too much debt, we may not be able to change jobs, move, make a wise investment, or even to serve when called upon by the Church.

If we want to be happy and successful in the future, we must work hard to maintain our financial freedom. There is something very comforting—even spiritual—about living well within our means. Many scriptures warn us that debt takes away our freedom. "The rich ruleth over the poor, and the borrower is servant to the lender."[5]

Live guilt free. It is impossible to feel guilty and remain happy. I don't believe we can ever reach our potential, have freedom and peace of mind, or be happy if we are harboring guilt. We cannot live in sin and be happy.

These five activities—building a good reputation, becoming a life-long learner, maintaining good health, preserving financial freedom, and living guilt free—will bring you choices and opportunities in the future that others won't have and will allow you to act quickly when opportunities come your way.

STRATEGY 3: ADD VALUE EVERY DAY

In the business world today, the time focus is shorter than ever before. Organizations used to focus on annual performance—how much profit they earned in a given year. They now focus more on quarterly and even monthly or daily performance. As the time focus becomes shorter, managers tend to make short-term decisions appear more profitable. As a result, employees start to be treated more like assets that can be bought and discarded than as individuals who must be invested in and nurtured.

To be successful in this environment, employees must find a way to add value to their work every day. It is no longer "what you did for me yesterday" that counts; rather, it is "what you can do for me today." When employees stop adding value to their employer that is at least as great as the amount of their pay, their job is at risk.

There are many ways to add value. You can develop an expertise or skill that others don't have, work harder than others, have a better personality and disposition than others, have better customer service skills than others, or learn and adapt to change faster than others. Employees who add the most value have jobs they truly enjoy.

STRATEGY 4: AVOID SELF-DEFEATING BEHAVIORS
So far we have considered three proactive success strategies—maintaining a sense of purpose and value beyond work, maximizing options and keeping nimble, and adding value every day. These strategies are only part of the formula for happiness and success—the other part requires the avoidance of self-defeating behaviors.

I have watched such behaviors destroy the careers and lives of wonderful and talented individuals. Examples of self-defeating behaviors include, but are not limited to: self-pity, lack of humility, inability to set and maintain priorities, selfishness, and sufferance from the "intent" syndrome.

Self-pity. No matter how talented and blessed, some people can't seem to avoid falling into the self-pity trap. They feel Heavenly Father and society have dealt them an unfair hand. Everyone else seems to have a happier family, better job, more money, or better looks and health. Self-pity is harmful but is particularly problematic in the business world. It is Satan's tool and primary way to induce discouragement—leading to hopelessness and unproductivity—which is deadly when you need to be adding value every day.

Fortunately, there is a quick remedy for this problem—service. Serving others helps divert attention from personal problems. I know a man who suffers from a severe wound he received in Vietnam. Instead of feeling sorry for himself, he spends every Sunday afternoon rocking crack cocaine babies in a hospital. It gives him a perspective that his problems really aren't that great and gives him a sense of fulfillment. We limit ourselves much more by what we think we can't do than by what we really can't do.

Lack of humility. The very moment we cease to be humble, we start on a road that makes us less valuable to others, less willing to listen and learn from others, and less fun to be around. And, as I said before, if we aren't continuously learning, we limit future options.

Inability to set and maintain priorities. We all know what is important, yet we still procrastinate. One of the greatest predictors of success in the workplace and even in the family is the ability to set priorities and follow through with them. When we fail to establish priorities, we let ourselves be driven by others like floating logs being tossed to and fro by the currents of a river. Setting and maintaining priorities will become even more important in the future as we juggle voice mail, email, pager mail, fax mail, land mail, and all other types of correspondence and communication at work and in our personal lives.

Selfishness. I know a man who, because of his selfishness, lost his family, his job (several times), and his friends. He is lonely because he doesn't know how to think about anyone beside himself. No matter how talented or educated we are, if we can't be a team player and let others receive credit, we will not be successful. Indeed, selfishness is a sure-fire way to fail in the business world.

The "intent" syndrome. People judge themselves by their intentions and others by their actions. For most of us, our intentions are much better than our actions. I intend to get up earlier, work harder, eat less, exercise more, and be a better father and husband. None of us is as good as we think we are, but we're probably not as bad as other people think we are.

When we judge ourselves by our intentions, we rationalize our shortcomings and give ourselves more credit than we deserve. We also tend to judge our colleagues and others more harshly than we should and ourselves too leniently. In addition, we tend to do less at work and at home than we think we are doing.

One of my research specialties is fraud. When you talk to someone who has committed fraud and been caught, he or she usually says something like, "I intended to pay that money back—I really did." We look at them and say, "You dirty, rotten crook, you stole money." You see, we judge these people by their actions; they judge themselves by their intentions. If we want to be successful, we must not let the gap between our intentions and our actions become too wide. We also must be careful not to judge others too harshly or give ourselves credit for more than we are really doing.

In conclusion, some current business writers believe that with all the uncertainty and problems in the world it will be harder to be successful and happy in the future. I disagree. With the right kind of preparation and the Lord's help, we will be able to navigate and maintain momentum in this topsy-turvy world, finding success and happiness along the way. With education and the knowledge of who we are and what is important in life and by maximizing options, adding value each day, and avoiding inhibitors of success, the changing world we face presents great opportunities.

ENDNOTES

1   Doctrine and Covenants 84:38.

2   Ecclesiastes 7:1.

3   Brigham Young, *Journal of Discourses* 3:203.

4   Doctrine and Covenants 89:18, 20.

5   Proverbs 22:7.

W. STEVE ALBRECHT

Steve Albrecht has been noted as one of the one hundred most influential accounting professionals in America for four consecutive years by Accounting Today *magazine. Albrecht, associate dean of the Marriott School, specializes in detecting business fraud and is a recipient of the Cressey Award, the highest honor given by the Association of Certified Fraud Examiners for lifetime achievement in fraud detection and deterrence. He has been named the outstanding accounting educator in the United States by the American Institute of Certified Public Accountants, the auditing section of the American Accounting Association, the Federation of Schools of Accountancy, and Beta Alpha Psi.*

Albrecht earned his BS in accountancy from BYU and his MBA and PhD degrees from the University of Wisconsin. He joined

BYU's faculty in 1977, after teaching at Stanford University and the University of Illinois. He is past president of the American Accounting Association and the Association of Certified Fraud Examiners. He serves as the U.S. representative to the International Federation of Accountants Education Committee and is a trustee of the Financial Accounting Foundation, the organization that governs both the Financial Accounting Standards Board and the Governmental Accounting Standards Board.

Albrecht has consulted with numerous organizations, including Fortune 500 companies, major financial institutions, the United Nations, FBI, and other organizations and has been an expert witness in some of the largest fraud cases in America. He presently serves on the boards of directors of five companies.

This speech is a compilation of several addresses given by Albrecht in 2002.

HONESTY AND INTEGRITY: ALWAYS THE BEST POLICY

by WILLIAM H. CHILD

*"A good reputation is your greatest asset
and makes sleeping easier at night."*

I want to compliment the Marriott School and faculty on your outstanding programs. I certainly want to congratulate you graduates. You chose a great school. I also want to congratulate your families—wives, husbands, and parents who have supported you throughout your educational process. You can be very proud of what you have accomplished. Now that you are receiving all these well-deserved congratulations and compliments, you have a challenge to make a difference in the world—to make it a better place. We have all been instructed: "Where much is given, much is expected."

I hope you will never quit learning. I admonish you to not only look ahead but also to look around at the many opportunities and challenges you have in the business environment.

We live in a world of greed and excessive corporate and private debt. CEOS and officers disregard shareholders' interests, cook the books, and distort income. CEOS are being overcompensated; there are accounting improprieties, stock option excess, etc. It's like the CEO who was interviewing a bright young accountant. He said, "I want to make sure you will fit into our organization. Tell me, what is two plus two?" The young accountant responded, "What do you want it to be?" The CEO responded, "Yes, you will be fine." That seems facetious, but apparently isn't as we look at Enron, WorldCom, Xerox, Qwest, Tyco, ImClone, Andersen, and others. These CEOS and companies committed dishonest, deceitful acts affecting people's financial security and future standard of living—they violated their shareholders' trust.

I recently read in a business magazine that accounting irregularities show \$1 trillion in hidden corporate debt. We often wonder why. Perhaps it's the pressure to succeed: to meet quarterly and annual analysts' projections, rationalizing that other corporate leaders are playing the same game, to increase stock prices, or to take advantage of stock options. As BYU graduates, the world will expect more of you. They will expect you to be honest and show integrity in all you do. I can testify that while it may not necessarily appear to be the best policy in the short term, it is always the best policy in the long term. What a sad situation when you leave a disgraceful legacy viewed by your family, friends, and associates.

WHAT YOU CAN DO

Obviously, you can't solve all business problems, but you can hope that integrity and honesty will come back in fashion. I recently read in *The Wall Street Journal:* "Wanted: Ethical Employees." Be an example to those you work with. Work for a company you respect—one with integrity.

Warren Buffett, owner of R.C. Willey, spoke at the Harvard Business School. The dean called him six months later and asked, "What did you tell these kids?" Warren said, "I just told them that they should work for someone they most admired. Why?" The dean responded, "They all want to go into business for themselves."

Remember that even one person can make a difference. Many of you are familiar with Samsung Electronics. In 1997, the CEO decided to go into the automobile manufacturing business. He was very excited about this venture. Some of his key advisors were not excited and didn't think it would work but didn't dare throw cold water on the CEO's enthusiasm. Three years and billions of dollars later, they decided it wasn't the business they should be in.

Many of you are already in business. You may have a suggestion or negative feelings about something, especially in the area of ethics. Speak up! In my forty-eight years of business, I have discovered that many large companies do some stupid things.

OPPORTUNITIES

You are lucky to be born in America. Only one out of fifty people is born in the United States. There are six billion people in the world. The United States has from 3 to 4 percent of the world population and more than 50 percent of the global GNP.

Most of the opportunities and advantages are in the United States. I have traveled to Asia and spent time in Indonesia, Vietnam, the Philippines, China, and Malaysia. In these countries their rich we would consider average and their middle class poor.

In China, workers are required to retire at age fifty, and then receive $9 a month from the government unless they are in private enterprise. Factory workers in China earn $2.70 per day. In Vietnam the average wage is $40 a month, which is $1.35 a day.

In Afghanistan, only 15 percent of the women and 35 percent of the men are literate. There are few educational opportunities and few modern conveniences. They have isolated themselves from the Western World. There are not many textbooks, publications, or scientific journals translated into Arabic. Those in the Muslim religion don't believe in paying or collecting interest—making it hard to get ahead in a world economic society.

CHALLENGES OF SUCCESS

You need to be patient, not complacent. It took R.C. Willey twenty-seven years to make the first million in sales or revenue, another four years to make the second million, and now we have $11 million days. We have $500 million in sales this year and are growing. A good work ethic and loyalty pay off. We promote ethical and loyal employees.

In a recent talk to high school graduates, Bill Gates said, "Flipping hamburgers is not beneath your dignity. Your grandparents had a different word for burger flipping . . . they called it opportunity. Television is not real life. In real life, people actually have to leave the coffee shop and go to jobs. Be nice to nerds. Chances are you'll end up working for one." He encouraged the graduates to be good, solid citizens.

Don't turn off your mind after graduation or after you go home. Always think! Good minds keep thinking. Don't follow the crowd or majority. They could be going down the wrong road, and the majority is not always right. Look at the Internet and the buying frenzy of the dot-com stocks and the IPO rampage. Many watched their neighbors get rich and joined the bandwagon. I know of one IPO that three individuals took public. It had a market value of $5 billion, and they didn't even own a fax machine—no physical assets, no earnings. Recently a dot-com company went public and raised $39 million, oversubscribed at $13 a share, and last time I looked, the stock was worth about $7 a share. They have never made a profit. You really have to worry about the investment community and the expertise of some investors.

ADAPTING TO CHANGE

Change is predictable. I am good at predicting the past but have a little trouble predicting the future. The small town of Syracuse, Utah, where we got our start, had a sign indicating a population of 268 people. There is no sign with the number of people today. They would have to change the number every day. It would be obsolete the day they put it up.

There has been significant change in some parts of the world. When I visited China eighteen years ago, everyone wore Mao uniforms; the streets were filled with bikes; there were hardly any cars; and they had only fifty busses in all of Beijing. There were no cameras, no freeways, and no private retail stores. The tallest building was six stories. Today's China has industry, fashion, automobiles, cell phones, freeways, and modern infrastructure. A sleeping giant has awakened.

The tragedy of 9/11 changed our country. Twenty men with box knives hijacked four airplanes and shut down America, particularly our financial markets. There have been immense changes in America and the world because of this.

It's important to predict future trends, such as the scooter craze. We sold more than twenty thousand in less than a year. Today they are not as popular. It was a short window. If you are alert you can see things coming. There have been many retail changes, with new competitors and new products. On the competitive side are Costco, Target, Home Depot, Sam's Club, and many specialty stores. On the product side, are faxes, email, Internet, voice mail, cell phones, and voice-activated cell phones. The challenge is to accept, adapt, and try to predict change.

ETHICS

Honesty is the best policy. You will be challenged. Take the high road. A good reputation is your greatest asset and makes sleeping easier at night. Your word should be your bond. If people were honest, we would live in a perfect world. There would be no need for lawyers, trials, courts, etc.

PRIORITIES IN LIFE

What is important? Your family, your faith, your profession, and your community service. These areas need to be in proper balance to feel good about yourself.

Money should not be your driving force; to have money is convenient. As the R.C. Willey Company has grown, our main focus has not been on how much money we make. Our driving forces are: constant improvement, service, and competitive prices. The profit comes as a by-product of better serving our customers. Obviously we have to control our costs, and by constantly increasing revenue we are able to grow and maintain our profitability.

There are no "get-rich-quick" schemes. They hardly ever turn out as indicated. Be careful in your investing, and adhere to sound business practices. It's better to make money the old-fashioned way: work for it.

ENJOY THE JOURNEY

You can all enjoy the American dream. If you adhere to the right principles, life can be wonderful. Enjoy every day and be positive. Make every day count. Try to accomplish something worthwhile each day. There are wonderful opportunities. Remember that honesty and integrity are always the best policy.

WILLIAM H. CHILD

William "Bill" Child serves as chairman of the board of R.C. Willey Home Furnishings. Under his management, the company has grown during the past fifty-one years from two to more than 2,600 employees and from a small six-hundred-square-foot store to twelve large stores, with annual sales of more than $600 million.

Child earned a BS from the University of Utah in 1954 and is now a member of the David Eccles School of Business Hall of Fame. He was awarded an honorary doctorate of business from Westminster College in 1998 and named the Marriott School's Entrepreneur of the Year in 1999. In 2002, he was awarded an honorary doctorate of humanitarian letters from Salt Lake Community College.

This address was given at the BYU Marriott School convocation 16 August 2002.

TRUE BLUE, THROUGH AND THROUGH

by SHERI L. DEW

*"Integrity is the foundational virtue
upon which all other virtues are dependent."*

n a recent conversation with LDS Church President Gordon
B. Hinckley, I described a difficult decision I had made at
work, one I should have made sooner. "President, I just
wish I were smarter," I confessed. Without missing a beat, he
replied, "Sheri, I wish you were smarter, too." Then, after pausing for effect, he added, "I wish we were all smarter."

I'd like to suggest there is more to being smart than I.Q. and
graduate degrees. I invite you to focus on a virtue that is just
plain smart because it will have as much impact on your happiness, peace of mind, career, and ability to fulfill your life's
mission as any virtue I can think of.

It is the virtue of integrity.

What I am about to tell you is nothing new. Breaches of integrity are as old as Cain and as recent as yesterday's news. Compromising one's integrity seems to be a common trap— and particularly for those who have strong aspirations. We tend to define integrity as honesty. And without question, it includes that. But telling the truth is just the beginning of integrity.

President Joseph F. Smith called integrity "the cornerstone of character."[1] He practiced what he preached. In fall 1857, the nineteen-year-old joined a wagon train in California en route home from his Hawaiian mission. One evening several outlaws rode into camp, threatening to kill every Mormon they could find. Most in the wagon train hid in the brush by a nearby creek, but young Joseph F. thought, "Why should I fear [these fellows]?" With that, he marched up to one of the intruders who, with pistol in hand, demanded, "Are you a Mormon?" Joseph F. responded, "Yes siree; dyed in the wool; true blue, through and through." At that, the hoodlum grasped his hand and said, "Well you are the [blankety-blank] pleasantest man I ever met! Shake hands, young fellow. I am glad to see a man that stands up for his convictions."

I love Joseph F. Smith's words: true blue, through and through. For the purpose of our discussion today, think of integrity as being true. True blue, through and through. True to yourself as a latter-day son or daughter of God. True to others, meaning you do what you say you will do. True to God, meaning you practice what you preach and you do what you covenanted to do here in mortality.

Living with integrity isn't always easy, but it is easier than the alternative. A case in point: I am a farm girl, and on a farm you learn to drive as soon as you can see over the steering wheel and touch the pedals—preferably at the same time. By the time I got my driver's license at fourteen, I was a seasoned veteran behind the wheel.

That first summer after getting my license, my job during harvest was to drive a grain truck from the field to the elevators, ten miles away via a dirt country road—a straight shot except for one stop sign before a two-lane, paved highway.

Now, it takes hundreds of yards to grind down through the gears and stop a grain truck. Each time I went through that long, tedious process, I couldn't help but think how much easier it would be if I didn't have to completely stop. Kansas is flat; you can stand on a tuna fish can and see forever. After indulging in these thoughts for a few days, I managed to convince myself and rationalize that it would be okay if I just slowed down but didn't completely stop.

I began to do this, and it made dealing with the stop sign much easier. Before long, not only was I not stopping, I wasn't doing much more than glancing both ways and barreling across the highway. I did this day after day, including one afternoon when I again ran the stop sign and proceeded down the dirt road toward our farm.

Five miles later, I looked in the rear-view mirror as I slowed to turn and, to my horror, saw a car with rotating red lights. After eating my dust for five miles, the police officer was not very cheerful. He demanded to talk with my parents. With red lights still gyrating, he followed me to our farm. Let's just say it proved to be a painful experience.

I learned three things that day: First, that with lightening speed, I went from complete observance to complete disregard of the law. Second, my demise started with a small crack in my integrity. The instant I talked myself into slightly breaking the law, I was on a slippery slide into full-scale disobedience. And third, there is actually no such thing as slightly breaking a law—whether a law of the land or a law of God—because even a slight breach of integrity opens the door for Satan. A halfhearted effort to be morally clean or to tell the truth is no effort at all.

On Mount Sinai the Lord didn't say, "Thou shalt not steal very often" or "Thou shalt only commit adultery a time or two." He said "Thou shalt not," clearly delineating the line between integrity and infidelity of any kind.

Integrity is the foundational virtue upon which all other virtues are dependent. It is the first rung on the character ladder. For where there is integrity, other virtues follow. Where there is no integrity, other virtues have no chance of developing. You either live with integrity or you don't.

It is not possible to develop a relationship, any relationship, with someone you can't trust. And trust is the keystone that holds every organization together—be it a marriage or a family, a business or a nation.

Ancient and modern prophets have provided patterns to emulate. Job set an example of integrity for the ages. Even after losing his wealth, his health, and his family, he declared, "Till

I die I will not remove mine integrity from me. My righteousness I hold fast, and will not let it go."[2]

The Prophet Joseph's vision of the Father and the Son consigned him to a lifelong crucible, but he never wavered: "I had seen a vision; I knew it, and I knew that God knew it, and I could not deny it, neither dared I do it."[3]

President Hinckley has also been a model of integrity. After Mike Wallace interviewed him for *60 Minutes*, I spoke with Mr. Wallace. Of the many things Wallace praised President Hinckley for, he seemed most impressed that the prophet had done everything in connection with the interviews that he had promised to do. When I later offered to show Mr. Wallace how I intended to quote him in President Hinckley's biography, he replied, "That's not necessary. You're a Mormon. I trust you." Do you really think that Mike Wallace believes every member of the Church is trustworthy? Of course he doesn't. His statement was a reflection of his experience with President Hinckley.

Indeed, anyone or anything that lacks integrity is unstable, as engineers will tell you. If a bridge, skyscraper, or building has structural integrity, it does what it was built to do. It isn't necessarily perfect, but under stress and repeated use, it does what it was built to do. If, on the other hand, a structure does not have structural integrity, it at some point fails, as was the case with the world's first jet airliner, the British-made de Havilland Comet.

When the Comet was introduced in 1949, the future seemed bright for jet travel—until three Comets disintegrated in flight, killing all aboard. The planes were grounded as engineers

worked feverishly to understand why they had operated flaw-
lessly at first, only to break apart later in mid-air. The engineers
set up a fuselage in a large pool and pumped water in and out,
simulating the effects of repeated cabin pressurization. At first,
the experiment revealed nothing, but then they learned that the
repeated stress gradually caused small cracks to form around
the windows, cracks that widened into gaping holes. The planes
could not withstand repeated pressure.

You and I live in a world filled with pressure—pressure to
succeed, pressure to get ahead, pressure to be smarter than we
are, pressure to conform. None of us are perfect. We all have
flaws. Under repeated pressure, how will we avoid cracks in our
integrity, cracks that over time could widen into gaping holes?
How can we stay true blue—to ourselves, to others, and to our
Father and His Son?

May I suggest six things that will help us fortify our integrity:

1. DECIDE TODAY, ONCE AND FOR ALL, THAT YOU WILL BE WOR-
THY OF TRUST—the trust of family and friends, colleagues and
business associates, and most of all, the Lord. The more the Lord
trusts you, the more knowledge and power He will give you.

The Holy Ghost is not able to inspire or endorse the words
or actions of someone who can't be trusted. Decide today, once
and for all, that you will be a man or woman of integrity who
can be trusted.

2. MAKE COVENANTS AND KEEP THEM. In other words, do what
you say you will do. This means keeping the covenants you

made at baptism and in the House of the Lord with precision. It also means being fair and square with others. Here is a sample checklist: Do you do what you say you will do, or do you regularly make excuses for not coming through? Do you rationalize taking advantage of someone if it is to your advantage? Do you give your best effort at work or just put in time? Is your behavior the same in the dark as it is in broad daylight? Are you true to those who have trusted you with their love and confidence? Are you living worthy of the man or woman you have married, and of the children who are and will be entrusted to your care?

Now is the time to learn to be strictly honest and commit yourself to a life of integrity. In future days you will face dilemmas far more complex than the ones I have listed, but these dilemmas can almost always be resolved if you are fair and honest and true.

3. STAND UP FOR WHAT YOU BELIEVE. In fact, look for every opportunity to do so. Don't be showy or loud about it, and please don't judge others in the process. It is not possible to denounce who you are and be happy. If you want to feel real joy, be true to who you are and what you believe. It is actually easier to stand up for what you believe than to not do so. When I was invited to speak about the family to a gathering of United Nations diplomats, I agonized over what to say. I ended up simply explaining that my parents had taught me that personal virtue was essential for a happy marriage and family, and that in my youth I had promised God to live a chaste life.

"It hasn't always been easy to stay morally clean," I admitted. "But it has been easier than the alternative. I have never spent one second worrying about an unwanted pregnancy or disease. I have never had cause to contemplate an abortion. I have never had the anguish of a man using and then discarding me. And when I do marry, I will do so without regret. So you see," I concluded, "I believe a moral life is actually an easier and a happier life."

I worried about how such a sophisticated, diverse audience would respond, but to my surprise they leaped to their feet in applause—not because of me, but because the Spirit had borne witness of the truth of that simple but profound message. The happiest and most successful people I know are those who have the integrity to stand up for what they believe.

4. EXPECT YOUR INTEGRITY TO BE CHALLENGED. Metaphorically speaking, be on the lookout for Potiphar's wife. Be ready, as was Joseph who was sold into Egypt, to leave your cloak in her hand and flee again and again, because Satan won't tempt you just once. Moses had to tell Satan to beat it four times before he finally left.[4]

Satan will try to find small cracks in your integrity that he can exploit and expand. Count on the fact that your integrity will be tested in large and small ways. This is actually a blessing, for you don't really know what you believe until your beliefs are tested. For example, you don't know if you can be trusted— with someone's feelings, money, influence, or power—until your trust is tested. In every test comes a moment of truth when you must decide what you stand for. Every time you choose to be true, your integrity will be fortified.

5. DON'T GIVE UP. Developing integrity is a lifelong process. I am fifty years old, and I have to work at this every day. The more determined I am to keep the commandments with exactness, the more aware I am of how far I have to go, and the more often I find myself repenting and trying again. Repentance and obedience are crucial to developing integrity—that is the pattern of life. When you do something that introduces a crack into your integrity, the Spirit will let you know so that you can repair it before it expands.

Recently a woman approached me in an airport and asked if I was the president of Deseret Book. When I nodded yes, she handed me a check and with emotion said, "Years ago I had a financial setback and could not pay a bill I owed your company. I have felt guilty ever since. Please take this so that my conscience can be clear again."

No one except the Savior will live a perfect life, and no one is perfected in a day. It takes time, work, and endurance to develop and refine our integrity. Learn to keep the commandments with exactness. Learn to delight in repenting and obeying. Don't give up.

6. COVENANT—or perhaps I should say, renew your covenant—with our Father and His Son to do what you came here to do. Doing what we agreed to do premortally is the ultimate expression of our integrity.

As in all things, the Savior is the supreme example of perfectly fulfilling His foreordained mission. He didn't do it for Himself; He was already a God. He did it for you and me.

Perhaps even the Savior didn't comprehend the depths to which He would be required to go, for there came that moment of unspeakable anguish when He pleaded, "Father, if thou be willing, remove this cup from me." But then, in the midst of that sheer agony, He added: "Nevertheless, not my will, but thine, be done."[5]

The Son of God was required to do what He was sent here to do. But at that moment of sublime submission, "there appeared an angel unto him from heaven, strengthening him."[6] Even the Savior of the world wasn't required to complete His mission alone, and neither are we.

We too made premortal commitments. You were sent now because you have everything it takes to deal with the world now. You have it in you to not only withstand the pressures of the last days but to triumph over them—but only if you are true to who you are and what you know, only if you can keep cracks from forming in your integrity.

Inventory your integrity. Look for cracks that may have started to form. Be honest with yourself about your past dishonesties. For the next thirty days take time every night to assess how you did that day. Were you true to yourself, to others, and to God in every situation? See if such an intense focus makes a difference in your decisions, your repentance, and even the way you feel about your life.

Turn your whole souls over to our Father and His Son. Express your deep desire to live with integrity and then plead for help. The Savior has the power to help you change. He will help you turn weakness into strength. He will make you better than you have ever been if you will let Him. I have felt His enabling power again and again. May we come to be more true than we have ever been before—true to ourselves, true to others, and most of all true to God, with whom we have made sacred and eternal covenants. May we be true blue, through and through.

ENDNOTES

1   LDS General Conference, 4 April 1897.

2   Job 27:5–6.

3   Joseph Smith History 1:25.

4   Moses 1:16–22.

5   Luke 22:42–43.

6   Luke 22:43.

SHERI L. DEW

In March 2002, Sheri Dew was named president and CEO of Deseret Book Co., overseeing the company's publishing operations, retail stores, Internet and book club marketing organizations, and seminar business. Fourteen years before, she served as vice president and then executive vice president of publishing for Deseret Book.

Dew was named in March 2003 by the White House to a delegation representing the United States at the United Nations' Commission on the Status of Women, an international commission designed to improve living conditions and opportunities for women around the world. She served as counselor in the General Presidency of the Relief Society of The Church of Jesus Christ of Latter-day Saints from 1997 to 2002.

A noted lecturer and author, Dew has traveled extensively, particularly to third-world nations, teaching, lecturing, and providing guidance for humanitarian, literacy, and family-focused projects. She earned her BA from BYU in 1977.

This speech was given at the BYU Marriott School convocation 13 August 2004.

SUCCESS AND PERSONAL PEACE: FIVE KEYS TO SUCCESS

by ALAN J. FOLKMAN

"Compounding produces more than simple isolated returns in everything we do."

S everal years ago I read a scripture that articulated a philosophy of life that I've always believed. This scripture not only has become my favorite passage but also my personal formula for success and peace. It is found in Doctrine and Covenants 90:24.

"Search diligently, pray always, and be believing, and all things will work together for your good, if ye walk uprightly and remember the covenant wherewith ye have covenanted one with another."

Although this was given in religious context, I think it applies broadly to all areas of our lives. I want to focus today on five ways we can apply this formula for success and personal peace.

These five applications are 1) be diligent, 2) pray always, 3) have faith, 4) walk uprightly, and 5) remember your covenants.

1. BE DILIGENT

Diligence is making our best effort, working hard, and doing all we can. The dictionary defines diligence as "earnest and persistent application to an undertaking; steady effort."

President Calvin Coolidge said, "Nothing in the world can take the place of persistence. Talent will not; nothing is more common than unsuccessful men and women with talent. Genius will not; unrewarded genius is almost a proverb. Education will not; the world is full of educated derelicts. Persistence and determination alone are omnipotent. The slogan 'press on' has solved and always will solve the problems of the human race."

This should be encouraging to all of us because it suggests that if we have not been born with natural beauty or talents, if we're not geniuses, or if we do not have degrees from Harvard, Stanford, or Wharton, we can still succeed with hard work, determination, persistence, and diligence. In business after business I have seen survivors rise to positions of responsibility and opportunity because they've been persistent in their effort and reliable in their performance over an extended period of time.

In the early 1980s, I met one of the country's greatest business leaders. His name is Sam Walton; his company is Wal-Mart. He was a dynamic leader who characterizes persistence and determination.

I recently read *Forbes* magazine featuring the richest four hundred people in America. Bill Gates was number one with

$63 billion. Larry Ellison of Oracle was number two at $58 billion. Before Sam Walton died in 1992, he divided his estate equally among his wife and four children. Each one of them was noted in *Forbes* with $17 billion. If you multiply $17 billion times five, that's $85 billion, meaning he created more wealth than the other two.

Let me share with you a couple of facts about his life that identify some of the characteristics that made him successful. He graduated from the University of Missouri and went to work for JCPenney in the early 1940s. He worked eighteen months and then joined the army. Once he was out of the army at age twenty-seven, he scraped together enough money to buy a small Ben Franklin variety store in Newport, Arkansas. His goal was to have the most profitable variety store in Arkansas within five years. At the end of five years, it not only was the most profitable store in Arkansas but also the most profitable variety store in the six-state region. He made a mistake, though. He didn't realize that he had signed a five-year lease that could not be renewed. He became a merchant without a store.

Determined to succeed in retailing, Walton took the fifty thousand dollars that he had saved and went looking for another store. Walton found Bentonville, Arkansas—a sleepy little country town of three thousand people—and opened Walton's Five and Dime. For the next twenty years, he opened and operated several five-and-dime stores. I think he got up to about nine stores by 1962, when he mortgaged everything he had to open the first Wal-Mart store.

Wal-Mart today has one million employees and is the largest retailer in the world. By the way, if you had invested two hundred dollars when he went public in 1970, the stock would have been worth $2.6 million when Walton died in 1992.

Did Sam Walton have earnest and persistent application to an undertaking? In his autobiography, he wrote:

"As I look back, I realize that ours is a story about the kinds of traditional principles that made America great. It's a story about believing in your idea, even when others don't, and sticking to your guns. I think more than anything else it proves that there's absolutely no limit to what plain, ordinary working people can accomplish if they're given the opportunity, encouragement, and set up to do their best. That is how Wal-Mart became Wal-Mart. Ordinary people joined together to accomplish extraordinary things."

Young people often have difficulty looking ahead to see how they will reach their goals. Will I make it to college? Can I get the grades I need to be competitive? Will I get the job I want? Will I ever get out of debt? Sometimes it's hard to imagine how we will get from where we are to where we want to be.

The realization of our goals often comes as a result of compounding. "The miracle of compounding" is a familiar phrase in finance; it's when you take an investment return of principle and interest and let it build on itself. Simple interest is payment on principle only; compounding is interest paid on accumulated principle and interest.

A dramatic example of compounding is the 1626 Indian sale of Manhattan Island in New York to a group of immigrants for

$24 in beads and trinkets. For more than 350 years it's been held up as the craziest sale in history. But let me tell you something about this $24. If the Indians had invested that $24 at 6 percent, it would be worth more than $35 billion today.

This is a result of compounding over a long period of time and doing small things consistently. What if they had invested their $24 at 8 percent instead of 6? The investment would be worth $30 trillion. It's amazing what rewards a little more effort produces over time.

What does compounding have to do with diligence and success? I believe that the miracle of compounding applies to all areas of our lives. Consistent and persistent effort in doing small things brings big results over time. Building upon results and then building upon what has accumulated is a powerful process. Compounding produces more than simple isolated returns in everything we do.

2. PRAY ALWAYS

The week after the Battle of Gettysburg, General Daniel Sickles, who had been in the campaign, asked President Abraham Lincoln if he was anxious during the Gettysburg Campaign. President Lincoln replied, "I had no fear." "How could that be?" asked the general.

Lincoln replied, "In the pinch of your campaign up there, everyone seemed panic-stricken, and nobody could tell what was going to happen. I went up to my room one day and locked the door and got down on my knees before almighty God and prayed to Him mightily for a victory at Gettysburg. I told God that if we were to win the battle He must do it, for I had done all that I could do. I told Him this was His work and that our cause was His cause and that we could not stand another Fredericksburg or Chancellorsville. Then and there I made a solemn vow to almighty God that if He would stand by our boys at Gettysburg, I would stand by Him. And, He did and I will. After that I don't know how or what it was. I just can't explain it; a sweet comfort crept into my soul that things would go all right at Gettysburg. And that's why I had no fear about you."

What a great example of how we should pray. Lincoln said his cause was just, he had done all that he could do, he needed the Lord's help, and he made a covenant with God to stand by Him and to follow Him. As a mutual fund manager, I prayed every day for discernment, for good judgment, and for the ability to make wise decisions. Prayer can help us in every aspect of our lives and truly brings peace to the soul.

3.   HAVE FAITH

The First Presidency said in the proclamation to the world, "All human beings, male and female, are created in the image of God. Each is a beloved spirit son or daughter of heavenly parents and, as such, each has a divine nature and destiny." And that destiny includes being an heir to all that God has.

We need to have faith that we are children of God with divine nature and individual worth. Knowing who we are and what we may become motivates us to self improvement. It's this faith and hope that helps us through the challenges of life. The dictionary defines hope as "a wish for something with expectation of its fulfillment; to have confidence, trust; a theological virtue defined as a desire and search for a future good, difficult but not impossible to attain with God's help." I believe that developing this principle of faith in our lives is the single most important thing we can do for success, because it provides the foundation from which we can do all things.

4. WALK UPRIGHTLY

The dictionary defines uprightly as "adhering strictly to moral principles; righteous integrity." In 1999, the Marriott School honored John Pepper, retired CEO of Procter & Gamble, as the International Executive of the Year. I heard him talk on the subject of personal leadership and character. He said the most defining characteristic of the most effective leaders he has known is personal character. What is character? I don't know if there is a definitive answer, but for me character begins with integrity. Be faithful in action to your most important core values, to your promises, and to your words.

Pepper quoted Ronald Reagan from a 1993 speech when he said, "The character that takes command in moments of crucial choices has already been determined by a thousand other choices made earlier at seemingly unimportant moments. It has been determined by all of the seemingly little choices of years past, by all those times when the voice of conscience was at war with the voice of temptation, whispering, aloud or internally, 'It really doesn't matter.'"

George Washington said, "I hope that I shall always possess firmness and virtue enough to maintain what I consider the most enviable of all titles; the character of an honest man." You may think integrity is a quality everyone has. Unfortunately, that's not true. It's a valued characteristic in the business world, widely admired and sought after in employees. It's one of those traits within the reach of all of us to develop in ourselves.

5. REMEMBER YOUR COVENANTS

I think covenants are a bigger part of our lives than we realize. One of the best books I've ever read on leadership is *The Winner Within,* by Pat Riley, the legendary coach of the Los Angeles Lakers and now coach of the Miami Heat. In his book, he describes how covenants were an important part of the Lakers' success.

The 1979–80 Lakers won the NBA championship in Magic Johnson's first year. Riley was the assistant coach. The next season the "disease of me" crept into that team, as Riley called it. Players complained about differences in salary and had personal agendas. They started complaining to the media, and the team began to unravel. And although the team was just as talented as the year before, they lost in the first round of the playoffs.

Early the following season the head coach was fired and replaced by Riley. The first thing he did was establish a core covenant with the players. Covenants can be written out in great detail or not written at all, but they are always clearly understood and supported, creating unity of purpose. He said every team member must decide consciously to uphold covenant terms that represent the best values: voluntary cooperation, love, hard work, and total concentration for the good of the team. The core covenant must spring from its natural leaders and spread throughout the team. The top producers have to be a source of that covenant. They have to monitor others and apply peer pressure.

Riley described what makes a constructive covenant. He said it binds people together, creates an equal footing, helps people shoulder their own responsibility, prescribes terms for help and support of others, and creates a foundation for teamwork. With the core covenant established, the Los Angeles Lakers won the NBA championship in 1982 and went on to become the team of the decade, winning the NBA championship four times and coming in second three times.

In his classic book, *Leadership Is an Art,* Max Dupre said the best management process is participatory management based on covenant relationships. The term describes a condition in which management and employees have clear agreement and understanding of the rights of the employees and the goals and objectives of management, and they work together for both.

Whether stated or unstated, we all work in an environment where upholding the covenants of work, family, school, team, or church organizations will bring greater success and satisfaction to the organization and to us. Most importantly, many of us have made covenants with God that are essential to our happiness and ultimate goals in life.

I believe that if we are diligent, if we work hard and do everything we can, if we invite the Lord's help, if we understand who we are and believe in our eternal destiny with faith in the application of the atonement of Jesus Christ in our lives, if we develop integrity and walk uprightly, if we do the best we can to keep the covenants we've made, then everything will work together for our good.

Faith is required to believe that. But if we follow the success formula, have faith, and do our best, we will feel inner peace, because we know that we've done everything we can. I've had many challenges in my life that appeared at the time to be road-blocks. With hindsight I can see that they were blessings. I've developed faith that things work out for our good, and there's a profound peace that comes with this understanding.

I will conclude as I began. "Search diligently, pray always, and be believing, and all things will work together for your good, if ye walk uprightly and remember the covenant where-with ye have covenanted one with another." I hope that we will all have the patience to let the compounding of daily, diligent actions work magic in our lives.

ALAN J. FOLKMAN

Alan Folkman is retired senior vice president and chief investment officer for Columbia Management. He joined the company in 1975 and served as portfolio manager for the Columbia Growth Fund, Columbia Special Fund, and the Columbia Common Stock Fund. Along with these positions, Folkman managed individual pension and profit-sharing accounts.

Folkman's professional career and expertise have been featured in several publications including Money Magazine, Smart Money, Fortune, Financial World, Barrons, *and* The Wall Street Journal.

He has also appeared on "Wall Street Week" with Louis Rukeyser and on CNBC's "Your Portfolio" with Bill Griffith and Jim Rogers. Folkman earned his BS in business management from BYU in 1967.

He gave this address 19 October 2000 as the Marriott School's Honored Alum.

WITHIN AND BEYOND OURSELVES: THE ROLE OF CONSCIENCE IN MODERN BUSINESS

by ROBERT C. GAY

"In the eye of faith, business is never a career but an ever-unfolding ministry."

The past couple of days our firm held annual meetings with our investors. During this time, my graduation gown was hanging in my office. A couple of my partners saw this and asked me if I was planning on changing the attire for our investor meeting. I told them no, but that I had the gown because I was going to be speaking with you today at this convocation. One of them then asked me, "What are you going to be speaking about?" I told him, "The role of conscience in business." He responded, "Well, that will be a short talk," and herein lies the issue.

Many years ago, just as I was finishing my doctoral program at Harvard University, my thesis advisor, a member of the finance faculty and an overseer of the Harvard endowment fund, called me into his office. He paced around the room a little and then said, "Bob, I don't know you real well, but well enough. I want you to stay here and teach." Then he paused and continued, "It's not because I think you're some great scholar who is going to make some breakthrough contribution, but because I know you can teach people here about God. I want you to tell our students about God. That's what I do in my office every day—they need and want to hear it." Up to this time, I had never spoken one word to my professor about religion. Yet, there I sat in this bastion of capitalism and rational Socratic methodology being told that the most important thing we needed to get into the lives of these would-be capitalists and future leaders of industry was the spirit of God. I think then, as well as now, I understand why—and this understanding is what I would like to share with you today.

When I was your age, the last thing in the world I wanted to do was to become a businessman. I served an LDS mission in Spain, and when I came home I just wanted to help people. My time and experiences at BYU and the University of Utah only reinforced those feelings. My desire was to be a seminary teacher, a social worker, or a psychiatrist—anything but a businessperson. I went to my dad to discuss the issue. He said, "I think a Harvard MBA would be great for you." Stunned, I accused him of believing the only thing that mattered in the world was money. He pragmatically answered me, "Son, all the love in the world and a few hundred thousand dollars are going to build the next chapel." The stark reality of that answer made me have an even greater dislike for everything to do with money or the corporate world.

I grew up in a brutal business environment. My father worked as the chief executive for one of the richest men in the world, Howard Hughes, and that world turned many lives upside down. I witnessed firsthand greed, deception, power struggles, and destruction of souls all for the sake of money. But perhaps what influenced me most is what I had seen in Mr. Hughes himself. For many years on Christmas Eve or Easter Sunday, Mr. Hughes would call and ask my dad to come to work. But this annual ritual was not what it appeared to be; Mr. Hughes invited my father to his home. When my father arrived, Mr. Hughes would simply say, "Bill, I just wanted to talk." Then after a couple hours of friendly conversation he would say, "It's Christmas. You better get back to your family." And I remember thinking to myself: "With all the money, with all the power, all the accomplishments, and even all the good he has done, he is both lonely and alone."

It was also during one of these reflective times that I learned another invaluable lesson about the role of the Spirit in such worldly matters as business and commerce—a lesson that would change me forever. My dad knew he wasn't ever going to win the battle with me about the MBA. In the end he simply said, "I hope you'll pray about this." I welcomed that challenge because I was sure God would not have me become a businessman. Nothing that crass would do. I prayed about it and though I did not receive a thundering revelation, my heart softened to the point where I decided it would not compromise my principles to visit Harvard. To appease my dad to some extent, I found a unique doctoral program that jointly bridged the economic programs of Harvard University and the Harvard Business School. I still refused to accept the idea of an MBA but felt it would be okay to do an interview for a PhD in a program where I could get a doctorate in economic development and center a career on the amelioration of world poverty.

I soon made arrangements at the school for an interview. There I had a most unusual experience. I had an early meeting and lunch with Harvard's most distinguished financial economist and my potential program advisor, John Lintner. He asked me many questions. Then, on the way back to his office, he paused and said he felt impressed to extend me an acceptance into the program. He said he would personally take my application through admissions for formal processing and that I would receive official notice in a few months—but he assured me that would just be a formality—I was in. And as clear as I am talking to you today, I heard a voice deep inside me say, "You are to be a doctor of business, not a doctor of medicine. You are to be here." I dropped all my other plans and applications. I could scarcely believe what I was doing. Yet I was very confident it was the right thing for me.

With the advantage of twenty-five years hindsight, I can now see the wisdom of the guidance I received. I have been blessed with the opportunity to be intimately involved in all the things my heart desired: job creation, poverty elimination, healthcare, education, youth rehabilitation, and helping build the LDS Church in many ways both here and abroad—all because of my work in business. Why do I share all this with you? For two reasons:

First, one of the most significant things I have learned in this life is that our very success and happiness depend not on doing what we like or think is best—but on doing the will of our Father in Heaven, no matter where that may take us and no matter how foreign it may seem to our own individual rational judgment of what is right or best. Our vision is just too limited. The scriptures remind us of this in Matthew 4:4: "Man shall not live by bread alone, but by every word that proceedeth out of the mouth of God."

While working on Wall Street, I had an experience that helped me learn the importance of yielding to the Lord's will. My firm, Kidder Peabody, was advising Macy's on a multibillion-dollar takeover of Federated Department Stores. We, the bankers, had been at the lawyers' offices day after day and were moving up the bid price by literally hundreds of millions without any real idea of true value. It became a contest of egos. In this tug-of-war, two unexpected things happened to me. I got a call from the chief financial officer of General Electric—a major shareholder of Macy's—and he asked me, "Bob what are we doing here? This deal doesn't make any sense to me." I said back to him, "You're right, it makes no economic sense. The best reason I can tell you why we're doing this is that you just bought Kidder, and if this deal goes through Kidder will make $15 million in fees." He said, "Okay, that's something I can finally understand. Thanks for being honest. I guess we should just keep pushing ahead." I thought, how crazy. Where was our sense of value? Kidder gets fees but the company ends up way over-levered, putting at great risk GE's multimillion-dollar stake. Massive job loss and store closure would also have to follow so the debt on the deal could be paid down. Then it struck me this deal wasn't the only crazy thing—I was also crazy. I was helping engineer this madness.

Shortly thereafter I was back at the lawyers' offices helping with negotiations. During a break, an investment bank colleague tried to convince me it was better to own a summer home in Paris than in the Hamptons because he could take the Concorde and spend less time traveling to a home in Paris than driving in the traffic on New York's Long Island Expressway. Then I heard that voice once again inside of me. It said, "Get out of this place. Take your experience and knowledge and move on." But then a practical voice said, "But if you leave you're going to lose the $400,000 bonus you'll earn for doing this deal, and you'll throw away your career and the millions you put yourself in position to earn over the long haul—millions that you can give to the Church or other great causes." The still voice returned, "If you don't leave now, you'll become everything you once despised." That possibility shook me to the core.

A few weeks later I left Wall Street and the money and went to a smaller investment firm, Bain Capital, where I became a partner with Mitt Romney, and started over. This made no sense at the time. Bain Capital was a fraction of the size of any house on the street. I had to take a huge pay cut to join. The firm had maybe fifteen employees and had done only a few small deals. It was impossible to know at the time that we would be able to grow our firm to a capital base of almost $14 billion today; or that we would be the means of creating thousands of jobs; or be the lynchpin behind thousands of other individual employees and a constant or often primary source of funding to more than fifty children's charities; or that it would bring me—and, for that matter, my partner Mitt—to positions that would allow us to exercise much more influence for good than could have otherwise been possible. Today it is easy, once again with the vantage of hindsight, to see the wisdom of the Spirit, which prompted me to leave the "street," over my rational mind, which told me any such move would be foolish and risky.

This experience and many others like it have taught me that in business, regardless of who we are or what we may believe, we will always be brought to crossroads. At these junctures, when the path is unsure, many will conscientiously ignore the call to faith and instead look only to their own wit, skill, and analysis to solve challenges. Because of this I look at each of you today with great concern. I know as sure as I am standing here that each of you is about to enter into a world where you're going to be unbelievably pressured to make decisions that will ask you to set aside the promptings of your soul and compromise principles you hold dear. In the words of my good friend Terry Warner, you will be sorely pressed to "betray yourself."

You will receive appeals to pride, prominence, prosperity, and power. You will be tempted to aspire, accuse, contend, and covet. Every day in your job someone will try to convince you that it's all about the money, but it will not be in those exact words. It'll be more like: "I got a 10 percent raise. What did you get?" or "I can't tell you how great getting the beach condo has been for our family." Others of you may find that you can't get the job or advancement or make the sale unless you pay some person some small favor or unless you join their party or club. And, as you protest the unfairness of the situation, there will be three or four others ready to take your place. Still others of you will feel emotionally empty from the loneliness of the road or the stress of the day and will find that, away from home where "nobody else will know or find out," there will be innumerable age-old invitations to fill that void. These calls to choose self over conscience will be endless.

I keep in my office a pair of cowboy boots of a man who sold his company to us. His wife gave them to me as a memorial to her husband who died of cancer just before we completed our transaction together. At one time, he had hoped to pass the company on to his family. But one son had wanted it all too soon and attempted a hostile takeover of his father while another son was sent to prison for defrauding the company. What started out as a family dream turned to a nightmare as selfishness took hold. The boots are my constant reminder of how easily things can fall apart when self becomes the primary driver.

At the other end of the spectrum is the need to guard against self-righteousness. You may recall the story in Mark 14:3–9 of the disciples who Christ rebuffed when they complained to him—with what the scriptures describe as "indignation within themselves"—about the oil that was being poured on his body and how much better it could be used if sold to help the poor. This should serve as a reminder to each us that when we go about our daily labors without the Spirit, ends and means can become confused, even when more noble aims are intended. What may seem to be good can actually end in unnecessary frustration and even harm.

Acts of the self-centered mind are a goodly part of the beat of modern industrial life and are like the "salutations in the marketplaces" referred to by Christ in Mark 12:38, which will always both flatter and tempt you. They are the very practices and challenges that so often make business a demanding world of raw selfishness aimed at ever-increasing profit. If not courageously resisted, this commercial environment will work to deafen you to all other voices. It will blur the lines between moral and legal correctness and try to make you doubt, compromise, or set aside your values. The recent events at Enron are a powerful witness to this very outcome.

Indeed, the Enron example alone should impress on you forever that you will not be able to stand if you rely solely on your own reason or desires. The more subtle reality—less visible to most—is that if you knowingly or passively accept your environment without question, just roll with the humdrum of the marketplace, or even if you rise to admired public reputation or exceptional Wall Street success, it will not matter because inwardly you will be conflicted. You will be unfulfilled and at odds with yourself because you will not be where you are supposed to be but rather in a spot where you risk your very soul. All my experience tells me this is so, and I can't even begin to tell you how many self-justifications you will be able to find to put your own voice over the voice of the Spirit. I believe President

John Taylor saw this when he spoke: "It matters very little what we are engaged in; it is impossible to do right without the guidance of the Almighty."

Second, I also share these experiences with you because I have found as you guide your life's decisions by the Spirit there is no such thing as careers—only fields of service—and that it does not make any difference whether you are a scientist, social worker, or business person. In the world of the Spirit, home teaching and business leadership are one. Moreover, I am sure as we gather here today, many at this university and elsewhere view us as distant and foreign from the real issues of life. Yet, please be assured, as C. S. Lewis once remarked in a speech to students at Oxford University: "The work of a Beethoven and the work of a charwoman become spiritual on precisely the same [basis], that of being offered to God, of being done humbly, 'as to the Lord.'"

One of the most moving and lingering memories I have in my business life began right here at BYU. In my freshman year I was asked to be the home teaching companion of an older student of Mexican descent, Ezekiel Sanchez. Zeke is the second oldest of sixteen children and was disowned by his father for joining the Church. He later dedicated himself to helping youth, in part because his childhood had been so tough. He partnered with Larry Olsen to start the outdoor survival program at BYU. He left the university to become a seminary teacher to Navajo youth and later became a director of training at the Provo MTC. But Zeke had a voice burning inside him that told him to leave Provo and go help troubled youth. He went to Arizona, where with Larry he cofounded the Anasazi Foundation aimed at touching the hearts of teenagers who struggle with heavy burdens.

One day while I was working in my office, a friend of mine called and asked me if I knew of any place that could help him with his daughter. I said I had an old friend whom I hadn't spoken with in more than twenty years, but who I knew was very involved in this area. I called Zeke and found out not only that he could help my friend, but I also discovered two other very important things. First, that Zeke and his partners had built a very successful program for helping teenagers, and secondly, that it was in severe financial stress—a burden I knew how to help fix. It soon became my privilege, once again, to be Zeke's companion in a mission that was no less noble than our first.

Now, I ask you this question: Why do you suppose I was assigned to be that home teaching companion some thirty-two years ago? Zeke and I surely didn't know what lay ahead for either of us, but I believe the Lord did, and I have come to believe that, in the eye of faith, business is never a career but an ever-unfolding ministry.

As you leave this campus, I hope you are filled with the desire to achieve the heights of your potential. Do not be content to avoid engagement. Honor the inspired motto of this university: "Enter to learn; go forth to serve." The scriptures also speak often and directly to this. In Doctrine and Covenants 58:26–28 we are encouraged to be actively engaged in good causes. In business this a special challenge, because the pull is toward all-consuming and uninspired busyness. However, I believe it highly instructive that King Benjamin in the Book of Mormon identifies his labor to lighten the taxes and the material burdens of his people as one of his great services to God. In Mosiah 2:14–16, we read how he made service a daily labor.

There is much that could be said about business and service, but as I have thought about it, one lesson that has always stood out to me is found in Moses 5:16. Cain—who the scriptures say "hearkened" to himself over the voice of the Lord—rejected the higher principle of service as his brother's keeper for the sake of gain. Modern revelation also cautions us about this temptation. We are to resist inappropriate emphasis on property and material gain. In Doctrine and Covenants 117:4, 6–8 we read:

"For what is property unto me? saith the Lord . . . Have I not the fowls of heaven, and also the fish of the sea, and the beasts of the mountains? Have I not made the earth? Do I not hold the destinies of all the armies of the nations of the earth? Therefore, will I not make solitary places to bud and to blossom and to bring forth in abundance? . . . Is there not room enough . . . that you should covet that which is but the drop, and neglect the more weighty matters?"

Consequently, as you go forward from here, the questions that you will constantly need to ask yourself are these: Will you set your heart more on personal gain or on being your brother's keeper? And if a brother's keeper, then what of your heart, might, mind, and strength will you consecrate on the daily altar of brotherhood? I believe you will find your response to these summons of the Spirit will be the defining force of your soul's character throughout the remainder of your life.

I had dinner the other evening with a close friend, a well-known alumnus of this school. I shared with him what I was going to speak with you about today, and he shared with me several examples of conflicts he had had, like being offered a million dollars to do a Coke ad, which he turned down—something that Coca-Cola just could not understand. Then he asked me, Bob, how do you really know when you're hearing the Spirit?" I leave with you this thought:

When I had my twelfth birthday, I went to the movies. The ticket for an eleven-year-old was twenty-five cents and for a twelve-year-old, thirty cents. Five cents meant an additional piece of candy. As I stood in the line, I rationalized away the fact that I was now twelve years old with the thought that I still didn't look any older than eleven. I then stepped up and bought the twenty-five-cent fare and got the extra candy. I was so proud of myself for having pulled this off that after the movie I ran home to tell my dad about my coup. He looked at me and said, "Son, would you sell your soul for a nickel?" It is a lesson I have never forgotten.

There is a voice within me and within each of you that is a transforming power. It constantly speaks to each of us, in its own unique way, to our minds and hearts every time we need to step forward or when we look to sell ourselves short no matter the price. It isn't so much that we can't hear it; it is more that we try to rationalize it away. My hope is that you hear that voice that is both within and beyond ourselves better than I did when only a few cents were involved.

As you look to that voice as your guide you will also find that how you and I individually respond to issues and challenges may be different because of our customized talents, tests, and missions—for in the world of the Spirit, every man arrives only, as Whittaker Chambers once observed, as he "hangs on the cross of himself." Honoring conscience, not conformity of thought or tradition, is what matters. Others will always be willing to make tough choices for you.

Your charge is to attune yourself and then exercise your God-given agency to act in accordance with His will. This choice is the cross each of us is expected to bear. As you take up that cross and prayerfully continue to follow the voice of the Spirit, your business labors may or may not bring you wealth or prestige, but I promise this: your work will bring you joy and happiness, and your life will not have been spent in a career, but in a ministry that will be a benediction to your family and to others in ways you cannot imagine. I think each of us would also be well served to remember Heavenly Father's caution and promise to those who obey or fail to obey His voice. In Mosiah 2:36–37, we find this word of caution:

"If ye should transgress and go contrary to that which has been spoken, that ye do withdraw yourselves from the Spirit of the Lord, that it may have no place in you to guide you in wisdom's paths that ye may be blessed, prospered, and preserved— I say unto you, that the man that doeth this . . . becometh an enemy to all righteousness."

In contrast in the Doctrine and Covenants 76:6, 10, we find this promise: "Great shall be their reward. . . . For by my Spirit will I enlighten them, and by my power will I make known unto them the secrets of my will—yea, even those things which eye has not seen, nor ear heard, nor yet entered into the heart of man."

Let me close now with this final thought from Elder LeGrand Richards, who said the following when asked to define what success meant:

"When I was eight, my father, who had just recently been ordained a patriarch, gave me a blessing. Among other things, he said that I had not come here upon earth by chance, but in fulfillment of the decrees of the Almighty to accomplish a great work, and then he defined that. All my life, I have prayed that if I didn't come by chance, that the Lord would help me accomplish what He sent me to do, so when my mission here on earth was completed, He wouldn't say to me: 'This is what we sent you to do, but you failed, and we had to raise up someone else to do your work for you.' True success, to me, is to accomplish the purpose for which the Lord sent me upon the earth."

That is my sacred prayer for myself, and it is also my hope and prayer for you. May each of you know that you are not here by chance. Great days and great success await if you leave here not only to go to work or to more schooling but to minister and attend to the Lord's purpose especially asked of you by the soul's light in your chosen endeavors.

ROBERT C. GAY

In July 2004, Robert Gay became president of the Accra Ghana Mission of The Church of Jesus Christ of Latter-day Saints. He was formerly a managing director and chairman of the Management Committee of Bain Capital, a privately owned investment firm. Before joining Bain Capital, Gay was an executive vice president of General Electric Credit Corporation Capital Markets Group and vice president in the Merchant Banking Group at Kidder Peabody.

Gay taught economics for two years at Harvard University, where he also earned a PhD in business economics and a Harvard Business School Division of Research Scholarship. He is actively involved with dozens of children's charities and humanitarian organizations such as Unitus and Forever Young. In 2004, Bob and his wife, Lynette, helped found BYU's Center for Economic Self-Reliance.

This speech was given at the BYU Marriott School convocation 26 April 2002.

AMBITION AND THE SOUL

by NATHAN O. HATCH

> *"Who you are has nothing to do
> with how successful you become."*

S everal weeks ago, I traveled to the north side of Chicago
to visit my son. I drove from downtown Chicago to
Lincoln Park, where he lives. As I turned onto Clybourn
Avenue, I suddenly encountered a scene that I hadn't seen or
thought of in years—the Clybourn Gospel Chapel.

The summer of 1967 flashed across my mind. I lived in the
Clybourn Gospel Chapel between my junior and senior year of
college. I spent that summer living with ten other students from
Wheaton College teaching classes and sponsoring sports activities for the teeming youth of that neighborhood.

I have many memories of that long, hot summer, most of
them involving intense interactions with other people: teaching classes, refereeing basketball games, and joining late-night

discussions with friends about important issues such as the meaning of life, the state of the church, and the dynamics of American politics.

Yet the most vivid memory of that summer was an evening I spent entirely alone. I remember, like it was yesterday, going up on the roof of that church where I could survey the lights of the entire Chicago skyline. That skyline was both alluring and frightening at the same time. It represented the world spread before me, in all of its vastness and complexity. I would soon leave the safe confines of a religious college to make my way. I knew how intensely I wanted to accomplish something, to make a difference. Yet on top of that building with the immense panorama of Chicago in front of me, I was never more aware of my potential insignificance, of how unclear my thinking was about what I wanted to do in life, and how insecure I felt about being able to accomplish anything noteworthy.

I spent that night wrestling with my own ambition. Why am I here? Will I make a difference? What are my gifts, my limitations? No one could answer those tough questions for me; and my own wisdom and experience seemed so limited.

Many of you may share the same intensity of concern about the future. My intent is to speak not only to those of you whose professional path is clear, but even more so to those whose future is uncertain. My subject today is: how do talented leaders, such as yourselves, come to terms with ambition? What I have to say may also apply to those of you who, like myself, are further along life's path.

This inner wrestling with personal ambitions can be intensified for three simple reasons. First, you do not know what you can accomplish and how far you can go. Many of you may feel like the young Abraham Lincoln, whose early career, without much distinction, left him with more than his share of self-doubt. In 1841, the melancholy Lincoln, doubting whether his life would amount to anything, confessed to a friend, "I would be more than willing to die, except that I have done nothing to make any human remember that I have lived." All of us aspire to use our God-given talents to do something for which others will remember that we have lived.

Second, it is not only self-doubt that shapes ambition. The fact that we are Americans also brings the issue front and center. The drive that you can make it on your own and be all that you can be is intense in this culture. We idolize self-made people, rags-to-riches stories.

In the United States, professional aspiration has replaced strict social class and family connection as the way we sort ourselves out. Professions reward hard work and performance rather than family connection. This appeals to our democratic instincts. At the same time, professions allow those with ambition to gain wealth and social standing—as the advertisement goes: put some distance between yourself and the crowd. We cherish social mobility and we expect social advance. In America, ambition is part of the air we breathe.

Those of us called to be followers of Christ also wrestle with ambition for a third reason: yearnings for accomplishment or success can be seen as the siren song of the world. We take seriously our Savior's call and example that to find life, we must lose it, that a seed must die before it lives. When the Zebedee family clamored for James and John to occupy the seats of honor in the kingdom, our Lord redefined, even inverted, the priorities of His kingdom. What constituted greatness and prominence was to serve, not to be served.

In volume one of the *History of the Church*, B. H. Roberts reports that Joseph Smith called believers to forgo vain and selfish ambition that he saw "mounting higher and higher." "The Church needed restoration because ambitious prelates of an apostate Christianity had gradually supplanted the religion of Jesus Christ." Instead, Joseph Smith called the faithful to follow "the Master," who had "discouraged ambition and had said that he who would be great among his followers must be their minister; and whosoever would be chief among them, was to be their servant."

The question you face today, and one that you will face the rest of your life, is: How do you relate the drive to make a name for yourself with the commitment to honor Christ, the name above all names?

Are we to nourish ambition as it wells up within our souls, or are we to kill it off? Does ambition constitute a virtue or a vice? Which of these American proverbs are we to heed: "Ride your ambitions to the skies," or "Ambition destroys its possessor"? How are we to discriminate among ambitions that are proper and those that are inappropriate?

In the past, ambition was condemned as unnatural, even immoral. The Latin word *ambitio* refers to those who would scurry about soliciting popular favor, drumming up votes, rather than allowing people to recognize true worth and character.

In the age of William Shakespeare and John Milton, ambition was often equated with the sin of Lucifer or of Adam and Eve—the unlawful desire to be of higher estate than God had intended. Many of Shakespeare's protagonists, like Macbeth, seek to reinvent their identities bequeathed to them and find themselves cut off from their true selves, their lives given over to shipwreck. "I charge thee, fling away Ambition," Shakespeare wrote in the play *Henry VIII*. "By that sin fell the angels." Ambition seemed like rebellion in a society that defined one's identity largely by birth and inherited status.

In the modern world, and particularly in America, by contrast, we have come to idealize opportunity, mobility, and progress. Onward and upward has been the prevailing American spirit. We idealize self-made figures like Abraham Lincoln, the rail splitter who went to the White House; Frederick Douglas, the ex-slave who became an articulate advocate for his people; Andrew Carnegie and John D. Rockefeller, who without education or status, transformed the scale of corporations.

Within your own tradition, The Church of Jesus Christ, there is a distinct pantheon of heroes who have accomplished notable things: business leaders like George W. Romney, J. Willard Marriott, and Stephen R. Covey; educational leaders like David Gardner, Kim Clark, and Gordon Gee; writers like Anne Perry and Brenda Novak; statesmen like Brent Scrowcroft and Orrin Hatch; and scholars like Richard Bushman and Laurel Thatcher Ulrich. One cannot imagine the sterling achievements of these individuals had not some blue flame of ambition burned brightly within.

Let me return to the central issue. It is easy to be caught in the vise grip of conflicting expectations: the drive to accomplish great things for noble purpose, on one hand, and to lose one's life that one may find it, on the other.

How does one cope with this abiding tension? Let me offer five pieces of advice.

1. DON'T ATTEMPT TO STIFLE AMBITION. Your finest hopes and dreams spring from the core of your very being. Those given great energy and drive are burying their talents if they do not use them. The process of suppressing ambition reminds me of Dorothy Sayers' description of trying to force a large cat into a small basket. "As fast as you tuck in the head, the tail comes out; when you have at length confined the hind legs, the fore paws come out and scratch; and when, after a painful struggle, you shut down the lid, the dismal wailings of the imprisoned animal suggest that some essential dignity in the creature has been violated and a wrong done to its nature."

The drive to accomplish is a good gift from God. The question is: What are its ends, what are its means, and by what measures do you judge success? It is inappropriate to simply stifle or suppress ambition itself.

2. THE AMBITIOUS PATH IS A DANGEROUS ONE. Ambition is not evenly distributed, as Joseph Epstein has noted, "Some people burn with it, while others, apparently wrapped in metaphysical

asbestos, never feel its heat." For those of you, like Lincoln, whose ambition is a little engine that never rests, you will trod a path of great opportunity and of great peril. Let me mention two reasons why ambition's road is dangerous.

A. Success rarely quenches ambition's thirst. Benjamin Franklin, an ambitious man if ever there was one, once noted that ambition never has the good fortune to satisfy us. Its appetite grows keener by indulgence. Two of the most famous people I know seem to hunger for achievement and recognition after having made it to the top. To me it seemed odd, and sad, that after all of their well-deserved achievements, they could not simply relax and revel in all that had been accomplished. At retirement age, one of these persons was bitterly disappointed at not receiving another presidential appointment.

B. Being driven to succeed often stems from a desire for belonging and appreciation, as C. S. Lewis once noted, our longing to be in the inner circle of things, to hear a profound "well done." Yet the style of ambitious people often repels those around them whose esteem and love they crave.

How often have you secretly wished that the person who breaks the curve, who wins the race, and who is most popular will be shown to have clay feet or will somehow stumble? I recall vividly the experience of the golfer Gregg Norman. He came to know the adulation of fans for the first time not when he was a champion, but after he experienced a devastating collapse of his game in the Masters' Tournament. Overt success easily backfires; seeking belonging and affirmation, it generates isolation and distance. Ambition is a dangerous path, because success rarely satisfies and ambitious behavior creates distance and resentment.

3. BE RUTHLESS AND SOBER IN SCRUTINIZING YOUR OWN AMBITION. At Notre Dame we had a wonderful assistant dean, who for forty years advised pre-law students. Bob Waddick was an old Navy salt who called a spade a spade; he deflated more pretentious and naive students than anyone I know. He would look at a student's ability, their record, and their work habits and tell them exactly what level of law school they should attend. Bob was so true in his judgments that law schools unfailingly accepted the students he recommended.

All of us need this kind of ruthless advice from time to time. The American myth that we can make ourselves anything we want to become sometimes allows our reach to far exceed our grasp. In the Christian community, where we are called upon to not think of ourselves more highly than we ought, it is even more imperative to form our identity in a process of careful listening and seeking advice.

It is also important to scrutinize professional ambition with respect to how it affects other dimensions of life. President David O. McKay offered sterling advice when he said, "No success in business can compensate for failure in the home"—a phrase that Dean Kim Clark of Harvard Business School often shares with MBA students.

The problem for people entering business and other careers is this: right out of school, the most formative influence in your life may be your profession. This world of work can easily embrace you with a grip more powerful and alluring than any-thing you have known in church or among friends and family. It is your law firm, your investment bank, your medical practice, your television station, or your consulting group that will con-sume most of your waking hours and exact your most creative energies. Your profession will tell you when to get up in the morning, what neighborhoods you should live in, what to wear to work, where to take clients to lunch, and what kind of orga-nizations you should join.

At a more substantial level, professional cultures will define what success means and what are acceptable values, patterns of behavior, and standards of conduct. In all likelihood, you will form close friendships with those who toil in the same profes-sional vineyard.

To excel today as a lawyer, a scientist, a research physician, or as an investment banker can easily demand exclusive loyalty. The time, energy, and commitment required to excel in these arenas make it difficult to balance work with other priorities: family, church, and community. The issues are even more acute for young women in religious traditions such as your own. Your education and ability draw you naturally toward professional excellence. At the same time you seek also to sustain religious commitments that make home and family the highest priority. Balancing these competing claims for men and women alike requires great wisdom and forbearance.

4. AMBITION SPRINGS UP IN THE MOST UNLIKELY PLACES—even in religious organizations and institutions. In these contexts,

ambition takes on more subtle forms—forms with their own liabilities. In a religious culture, many will never admit to being ambitious even if others may perceive a pattern of ambitious actions. In a business organization, it is often a liability not to express ambition for more responsibility. In a religious one— and in most universities—overt interest in leadership is generally frowned upon.

Yet we would be naive to act as if ambition, our own and that of our peers, were not a powerful force in shaping religious organizations. For those of us who work in places like Notre Dame or BYU, we must give extra scrutiny to our own ambitions. We must check and channel those powerful subterranean currents of ambition, even if in public they are rarely acknowledged. We must ensure that our own dreams for an organization are directed to the common good. We must serve not just in word but also in deed.

5. WHO YOU ARE HAS NOTHING TO DO WITH HOW SUCCESSFUL YOU BECOME. Our culture forges a tight link between success and identity—your accomplishments give you worth.

Modern professional life reinforces a sense that success is the measure of all. Professions are a meritocracy of good works. Right diagnoses will lead to a successful cure; sound legal argument will win the case; correct design of a bridge will make it withstand traffic. Professions reward competence and penalize incompetence. That is all well and good. Who can argue with it?

The problem is that success easily becomes the measuring stick for everything. Life becomes a bookkeeping scheme of merit and reward. We applaud success in ourselves and take great comfort in it, and we rank other people accordingly. Professions reinforce our love of being winners and of rubbing shoulders with other successful types. All too easily professionals get to the top of the heap, congratulate themselves, and look down upon others.

The problem with this ethic of success is that it stands on a collision course with how God treats His people and how we are to treat each other. Christ did not come into the world to save only those who were helping themselves. He came to rescue those in need. The clarion call of Joseph Smith and Brigham Young was for a reconstituted church that would not be a respecter of persons but would embrace everyone and take care of everyone. Success is dangerous for the Christian, because in its grip we can easily judge each other and ourselves by its yardstick rather than by standards of love and acceptance.

All of us, those who are driven and those who are relaxed, those at the top of the class and those who have struggled, those who relish the future and those who are gripped with fear—all of us derive our tremendous worth because God in Christ calls us sons and daughters and welcomes us into the wonderful banquet of His kingdom. Our identity rests not on our fickle ability to climb the organizational ladder but in the embrace of God and His people. Any of our own achievements will pale before these priceless treasures.

I have attempted to bring some perspective to the reality of ambition in our lives. I have suggested 1) that ambition is not something merely to be suppressed; 2) that ambition is a dangerous path, both because success rarely slakes its thirst and because the ambitious person often repels those whose friendship and acceptance we crave; 3) I have suggested that ambition needs regular scrutiny; 4) that it is a reality even in religious contexts, even if its form is more latent than overt; and my final point, which I wish to underscore, is that 5) our identity is not based on how successful we may become.

NATHAN O. HATCH

Nathan Hatch, one of the most influential scholars of American religion, was appointed president of Wake Forest University in July 2005. Before joining Wake Forest, Hatch spent most of his academic career at Notre Dame, where he served for ten years as provost, the university's second-highest-ranking official.

Hatch was appointed to the Tackes Chair in 1999 and was a Notre Dame faculty member since 1975. His book, The Democratization of American Christianity, *was chosen in a survey of 2,000 historians and sociologists as one of the two most important books in the study of American religion. Appointed by President Clinton, Hatch is a member of the National Council on the Humanities, the twenty-six-person advisory board for the National Endowment for the Humanities.*

Hatch graduated summa cum laude *from Wheaton College in 1968 and earned his master's and doctoral degrees in 1972 and*

1974, respectively, from Washington University in St. Louis. He has held postdoctoral fellowships at Harvard and Johns Hopkins Universities.

He delivered this forum address in the Marriott Center at BYU 27 March 2001.

BECOMING PEOPLE OF INTEGRITY

by NED C. HILL

*"The integrity of a person is the
measure of how consistent that person is
from the inside to the outside."*

I submit to you that one of the most important things you can do in this life is to become a person of integrity. The world desperately needs people of integrity. What do we mean by the concept of integrity? Integrity of a metal means that the metal has certain measurable qualities throughout. If it lacks integrity, the metal has a flaw that may not be seen by the naked eye but may cause the metal to fail when pressure is applied. Integrity of a tool means that the tool will perform in accordance with its specifications. It has consistent qualities that can be measured and tested.

The integrity of a person is the measure of how consistent that person is from the inside to the outside. A person of high integrity is who he or she claims to be. Such a person of integrity

performs under the pressure of real and demanding situations—
not just when it is easy. It's one thing to be a ladder standing
in my garage; but the real test of that ladder is when it has to
perform under pressure. Likewise it is relatively easy to claim
to stand for certain values when the pressure is off—but much
more difficult to live those values when life's pressures come.

Let's be more specific to you and me. It is relatively easy
to proclaim to be a follower of Christ. The person of integrity, however, will not only proclaim outwardly to follow the
Savior but will, under the pressures of life, demonstrate attributes of the Savior on a consistent basis, day in and day out.
Internally that person of integrity will be Christlike. No matter
what the challenge is, principles taught by the Savior will come
through—whether in a group or alone, in public or in private,
on Sunday or on Monday, in church or in a sales room.

The Lord, speaking about Joseph Smith's brother, said these
loving words: "Blessed is my servant Hyrum Smith; for I, the
Lord, love him because of the integrity of his heart."[1] Loyal
and true Hyrum! He was faithful to the gospel and completely
devoted to the Prophet Joseph throughout both their lives. He
was tried and tested and proved faithful under all challenges—
even at the very end when he joined Joseph in sealing his testi-
mony with his blood in Carthage, Illinois.

The Lord highly values integrity. He promised great blessings to Solomon if he "will walk before me, as David thy father
walked, in integrity of heart."[2] Unfortunately, David did not
retain his integrity throughout his life. Another prophet, Job, is

held up as a man who "holds his integrity" in spite of numerous challenges.[3]

There are many examples of people of integrity (and some who lack it) in modern times. May I illustrate from my own observations related to the business world? There are many lessons we can learn from these examples.

I recently attended the funeral of my friend Lowell Benson, executive vice president of the O.C. Tanner Company and their chief buyer of diamonds and gold. He was also a stake president in Salt Lake City and a great friend and graduate of BYU and the Marriott School. His funeral packed a large stake center. I was curious to see that people attended from the diamond capitals of the world: Antwerp and Johannesburg. Their messages were read at the funeral. I paraphrase, "We knew Lowell as an excellent man of business. More importantly, he was a man of integrity. He drove a hard bargain, but he could always be trusted to keep his word."

Jon Huntsman, Sr., is one of the most successful businessmen in America. He has founded a number of companies in the republics of the former Soviet Union. Two of his former employees were in my MBA class at BYU and told me of the box factory he created in Russia to help this emerging economy. Initially the company was told it would have to pay a certain tax rate on boxes sold to Russian customers and a much lower rate on boxes shipped for resale to other former republics. After the company started producing boxes, a tax administrator came and informed the company that the rates were being increased on the exported boxes—to a point that made the company completely unprofitable. However, the official said, if certain amounts could be paid under the table directly to the tax official, he could "take care of them." It is Jon Huntsman's policy never to pay a bribe. He never has; he never will. The official was insistent. Jon Huntsman decided to sell the factory to local management for $1 rather than pay a bribe. He lost his investment of millions of dollars, but he would not compromise his integrity for money.

Recently one of our top BYU MBA graduates accepted one of the most lucrative jobs of the year with a prestigious company. He and his wife moved to a large city and were enjoying the prospects of a rapid move up the success ladder. But he was asked to engage in business practices that compromised his integrity. His supervisor wanted him to make significant misrepresentations to customers. He approached his superiors and told them he could not do what they were asking him to do. He was fired. He spent several months out of work. Fortunately, he finally did get another very good job—even better than the first.

An accounting clerk at a large university became a respected member of his profession—even holding a high office in his professional association. He was active in his church and community and had a good family. One day he discovered how he could take small amounts from the university without anyone noticing. He told himself that he was underpaid anyway—and besides, he would only use the money a short while and then return it. But the next month, more money was needed. Just a little more would not matter—he'd pay that back, too. The months stretched into years. The total amount taken swelled to several hundred thousand dollars. Then came the day when an audit uncovered his fraud. His reputation was shattered. His career came to an end. His family disintegrated. Ties with his church were broken. Where once he was a respected member of the community, now he was a common criminal unworthy of the trust and confidence of any employer.

Two partners in an e-commerce start-up company negotiated a contract with a large company to provide their customers seminars on this new field. The large firm provided seed money to help the small company get started. A few months later, the partners realized that, under the terms of the contract, they owed the large company about $40,000. If that amount had to be paid immediately, the small company would have to shut its doors. The original intent of the contract would not have required payment, but the wording of the contract was such that the small firm owed the $40,000. At the same time this was discovered, the large company changed the manager who was responsible for the contract. He probably did not know of the contents of the contract nor of the intent. The two partners had a choice—if they told the new manager about the $40,000, they could have to pay it and lose their company. If they did not tell him, the new manager may never find out and they could stay in business. The partners said to each other, "It's only money. We built our company on the principles of integrity. We can't let money stand in the way of that principle." They called the new manager and explained the situation. He asked for a few days to consider the matter. He later called back and said, "You have been men of integrity. We find that a rare commodity in today's business. Because we now know we can trust you, we want you to keep the $40,000." That year, the small company generated more than $1 million in business with the large company, and the relationship continued at that level for many years.

A father was preparing his taxes late one night. He had assembled all the appropriate records and worked hard to determine what he owed the IRS—never the most joyful experience in life. When all was computed, he found that he qualified for a small refund. But then he suddenly remembered a transaction. He had been paid for one fairly large job in cash. No records were made of the transaction. He realized that the IRS couldn't have received a report of this income and likely would never know about it. Reporting it would cost him more than $1,000 in state and federal taxes—a sizable amount to his young and growing family. But then he thought, "I am a man of integrity. This is a small price to pay for resting well at night knowing I have been honest." He had to take out a short-term loan from the bank, but he paid the extra taxes and slept well.

Now, what can we learn about integrity from these stories? You probably drew your own conclusions. Let me suggest a few of mine. First, integrity usually extracts a price. To be a person of integrity we must be willing to pay that price. It cost Jon Huntsman literally millions of dollars. It cost the MBA student his job. Neither had any hope of monetary reward for living with integrity.

Second, living with integrity may bring recognition from the world—but not necessarily. People came from Belgium and South Africa to honor Lowell Benson for his life of integrity.

The start-up company was rewarded with millions in revenues because they established a relationship of integrity with a customer. A recruiter told me the other day that his firm came to BYU to find employees because he knew they were well-trained and had integrity. But worldly recognition is not necessarily the case nor should it be expected. The young father was not rewarded with public acclaim but with a clear conscience, peace of mind, and a good night's sleep.

Third, the decision to live with integrity is not always the easiest path to follow—especially if one measures decisions by worldly standards. The MBA student's decision to leave a prestigious firm over an issue some might consider "just business" would not have been considered wise by worldly career consultants. Sometimes living with integrity brings pain.

Fourth, people generally don't set out to intentionally lose their integrity. Loss of integrity comes usually very slowly, a small step at a time. The accountant did not intend to defraud his employer, only to be "fairly compensated." He just took a little at first. He always intended to pay it back. He never considered himself a "bad man" or one who lacked integrity.

Fifth, loss of integrity can bring devastating consequences that go far beyond the incident where integrity is compromised. The accountant lost everything he valued: his family, his church, his career, his respect in the community, his friends and, for a time, his freedom. Think of the ills in our society caused by a lack of integrity. Families are torn apart when a husband or wife lacks integrity in upholding marriage covenants. Children become alienated from parents when there is lack of integrity in the family unit. Think of the billions lost each year in the retail trade in the United States due to shoplifting. It is a sad note that for most retailers, the majority of their losses come from employees rather than dishonest customers. And think of further billions in aid that is sent to underdeveloped countries in Africa and elsewhere. What a tragedy that such a high percentage is siphoned off by corrupt political leaders rather than benefiting the people who so desperately need this assistance.

Now we may not be able to exert much influence on some of these very large problems—but we can start by changing ourselves and maybe, just maybe, that will help the world be a little bit better. How do we know of we are becoming a person of integrity? Let me give some possible questions to ask ourselves to determine if we are on that road to integrity. These are the small things we must do over and over to eventually become great souls of integrity.

Am I honest in school assignments? Would I ever pass off work as mine when actually it was created by another? Would I ever take from another that which I should not without fair compensation—for example, do I use pirated computer software? Do I make illegal copies of copyrighted materials such as music or published articles?

Is there integrity in my business dealings? If I received more than I should have in a business transaction, would I return the excess? Would I ever represent my product to a potential customer as something it is not?

Am I honest in my taxes? Am I honest in my tithing and fast offerings? Am I honest in my relationship with my employer?

Can I be counted to provide an hour's work for an hour's pay? Can I be completely trusted with my employer's assets?

Can I be trusted with another's reputation—in other words, can I be trusted to avoid gossiping about another? Am I a true friend when that friend is not around?

How do I behave when no one is watching, when no one can find out what I did?

When I give my word, can it be relied upon implicitly? When I make a commitment, do I keep it? When I make a sacred covenant, do I uphold my vows?

While it takes years to become a proven person of integrity, it is so easy to lose integrity—and so difficult to restore it. Nephi warned us that it is easy to "lie a little, take the advantage of one because of his words, dig a pit for thy neighbor; there is no harm in this" we might be tempted to say. [4]

How do you know when you are losing your integrity? The still, small voice will tell you, the whisperings of the Holy Ghost. I promise you that if you listen and heed its warning, you will know clearly if you are getting on the wrong track and need to make a course correction. In contrast, if we ever become too busy or too insensitive to listen, then we may find ourselves as Laman and Lemuel. Nephi said of them: "And he hath spoken unto you in a still small voice, but ye were past feeling, that ye could not feel his words." [5]

I suggest to you that, while we have many examples of people of integrity all around us, we must look to the Savior to see the perfect example of a man of integrity. Throughout His life, He never wavered from doing His Father's will. He was the same inside and out—what He preached was exactly what He practiced. He never feared nor sought the opinions of the world but steadfastly carried out His divine mission. He stood ever ready to pay whatever price His integrity demanded—ultimately paying that enormous, incomprehensible price for us in Gethsemane and then on Calvary. He refused to "shrink" but drank from the bitter cup that was placed before Him.

I know He lives and leads this Church today through a living prophet, President Gordon B. Hinckley. What a great blessing we have to have this great prophet of integrity leading us today—both the Church and this wonderful institution, BYU. I testify that those who serve with President Hinckley—his counselors President Thomas S. Monson and President James E. Faust, the Quorum of the Twelve, the Seventy—are also men of complete integrity, worthy of our trust and support. I have had the blessing of seeing these men close up and testify of their divine callings. I testify that Joseph Smith was a great man of integrity, the prophet of the restoration.

I know that it is worth whatever price we must pay to become people of integrity. The world needs you to become such a person. The Lord needs to rely on us as people of integrity so that we may bless His children. Oh, how sweet it would be to have the Savior say of you and me:

"Blessed [are you] for I, the Lord, love [you] because of the integrity of [your] heart."[6]

ENDNOTES

1   Doctrine and Covenants 124:15.
2   I Kings 9:4.
3   Job 2:3.
4   2 Nephi 28:8.
5   1 Nephi 17:45.
6   Doctrine and Covenants 124:15.

NED C. HILL

Ned Hill has served as dean of the Marriott School since July 1998 and has been a part of BYU since 1987. Before his appointment as dean, he served for two years as assistant to BYU President Merrill J. Bateman, assuming responsibility for strategic planning in the areas of facilities and space management, distance learning, information systems, and assessment. Before joining the administration, he chaired the Marriott School's Department of Business Management.

Hill is a widely published author and frequent speaker on the subjects of treasury management, electronic commerce, and personal finance. He was founder and senior editor of EDI FORUM: The Journal of Electronic Commerce *and has written four books and more than seventy professional articles. For several years he served on the Information Technology Commission for the State of Utah, and he has been a regional director of the Financial Management Association.*

Hill holds a PhD in finance and an MS in chemistry from Cornell and a BS in chemistry from the University of Utah.

This chapter is adapted from a speech given at a BYU–Idaho convocation 28 November 2000.

TO FAMILY, BUSINESS, AND HUMANKIND

by JON M. HUNTSMAN, SR.

> *"No one achieves anything*
> *without paying a price of hard work, integrity,*
> *emotion, and years of effort and sacrifice. "*

I have been asked to address some aspects of business that deal with family and humankind. I'd like to quote from two great Americans. The first is Thomas Jefferson. He made this statement: "I deem it the duty of every man to devote a certain portion of his income for charitable purposes; and that it is his further duty to see it so applied as to do the most good of which it is capable."[1] I've always had that particular expression on my desk to remind me that we not only have a duty, we have an obligation, irrespective of our levels of income, to be concerned with those around us, to be concerned about the humanitarian nature of life, and to apply as much as we're able to the furthering of humankind and human souls. The second thought is by Andrew W. Melon, one of the great industrial pioneers in America who helped shape much of our economic frontier. He made this statement dealing with business: "If the spirit of business adventure is killed, this country will cease to hold the foremost position in the world." The combination of business adventure on the one hand, and our duty, our obligations, our solemn purpose to help those in need on the other hand, provides the basis for a few thoughts I would like to present to you today.

All of us are members of a family. Maybe the family is one, maybe it is two, maybe it is three or more. Whatever may be the case, I would like to make a few suggestions that will help us as we develop ourselves and our families in understanding more fully this great "business adventure" that is so critical to maintaining our foremost position in the world.

Our Church has always preached and taught that we would be better served in our families if we could have a family night where some aspect of the gospel is presented. A night when we interact one with another, and where we share stories that lift the human soul. May I suggest that if a family night helps develop our spiritual roots, understanding, and love with one another, think of what calling the family together would mean if we discussed our businesses and educated our spouse and our children—or perhaps our parents—on what it is we are doing in the world of business. A time to talk about matters such as integrity and honor and having one's handshake be one's bond; to explain to our children what it means to make a contract and how binding it is to shake someone's hand and how legally binding that

becomes upon the person who has extended his hand, irrespective of a written contract.

Many years ago, as our company was going through the
embryonic start-up years, it was necessary, in order to pay
some early debts I incurred, to sell a portion of our company. I
found an appropriate buyer and negotiated a price to sell where
I would keep 60 percent of our business and sell 40 percent. We
since have repurchased that 40 percent some years ago, but at
the time, and in most start-up situations, additional capital was
required—and this was no different. After major discussions
with the chairman of a New York Stock Exchange company,
I agreed to sell him a 40 percent interest in our business at a
fixed price. Over the next several months much delay occurred.
During the process of that time, our contribution margins accel-
erated. The volume of our business activity quadrupled and our
profits went up five-fold to the point that when it came time
to sign the document, the value, instead of being $53 million,
was $250 million. The chairman of the company said, "Jon, you
have an important decision to make. You can either make a great
deal of money from me since we have not signed anything, or
you can go back to your original handshake." Well, no matter
who you are, or what amount of money you may possess, you
always have to think, just for a minute, about what's being said
or what's being asked. But without hesitation I was proud and
honored to step up and say, "Mr. Campan, I shook your hand. I
made an agreement. The price will be $53 million. That's what
we agreed to six months ago." I must tell you that throughout
the last twelve to fifteen years there have been many times I

have wondered, "What about that $200 million?" That's a for-tune, a mammoth fortune. I let it slip away. And on the other hand I say, "My children are all in the business. They know their father; they understand an agreement. If it was for $53 million or just $53, the principle is still the same. A deal is a deal. A handshake is a handshake. Integrity is integrity." Often, in today's world, we are of the opinion that whatever we can get is fair, and whatever we can squeeze out of somebody is okay and ethical. Correct principles, taught in a family night setting, are as vital a part of family night and family activities as any aspect of life we will ever encounter.

Throughout our marriage, Karen and I have held our family nights on a very regular basis. It didn't matter whether I was in the White House, as I was for a couple of years; it didn't mat-ter whether we were serving a mission, which we did for three years; it mattered not if we were running global businesses; our family nights were very important. A significant part of each family night was conveying an understanding to our nine chil-dren of what their obligations were in dealing with others and in dealing in the important world of business. I had no idea that someday I would be working with all of them. One is a consul-tant and eight of them are full-time with the business, including the sons-in-law. I had no idea the words I was teaching would be the code of conduct, the code of ethics we would someday be living.

Many people say to themselves, "I can't buy this particular home, or I can't take this particular family outing because it's difficult to afford it. We don't have the money, and it just won't stretch that far." May I suggest to you it is very difficult to lose money investing in our families. It is very difficult to lose money by going on family outings and doing events with the family. We lose money by poor investments. We don't lose money by making critical, essential, and timely investments in family outings. How many times have we said to our families, "I can't afford that," when in reality what we're saying is, "I've lost on some poor investments in real estate or business, and therefore I can't do this for my family." We must separate very distinctly a business investment from a family investment. I've always tried to teach our children they will never go broke spending what money they have on their family needs as opposed to business investments, which often can be lost. We should never confuse the two.

Many of us often count the other person's money. We say to ourselves, "How much is he or she making on this business proposition?" We should always think first and foremost, "What am I receiving? Is it fair and ethical and honorable?" Let's not waste our emotion, our feelings, our time, our sensitivities on worrying about how much somebody else receives. I don't know how many times I watch in amazement as honest and wonderful people exert enormous emotion and tribulation in not cheering for the other guy. What a joy it is to cheer for someone else's success. We don't need to tear the other person down to build ourselves. What a great honor it is when people say, "Brother Huntsman, congratulations. I was cheering for you." They don't have any idea how much I appreciate that, or what that means. We've had our roadblocks. We've had our share of adversity. We've had years of struggle to bring our company where it is today and our level of income where it is today. We've had to pay the price. We've tried to do it quietly. We've tried to do it within the bounds of propriety and integrity, but no one achieves anything without paying a price of hard work, integrity, emotion, and years of effort and sacrifice. It doesn't fall in your lap by luck. We've tried to teach our children to cheer for others, to be happy when they're successful. Don't waste your emotions and your energy on anything that could be negative. You need every ounce of energy you have to build your own business.

I had an interesting professor at the Wharton School when I was an undergraduate. His name was Dr. Chester Cline. Dr. Cline would enter the classroom and always say, "Remember students: buy low, sell high." Every single day. Years after, I looked back on my education at the first business school in America, the Wharton School at the University of Pennsylvania, and I remember first and foremost Dr. Cline's remarkable advice. Buy low, sell high. Hard to do. Difficult to do. Why is it so difficult? May I make a suggestion? It is often difficult to make the right investment because we are impatient. We do not take the time to wait for the proper cycle to come around, for the proper investment to come our way, for the proper situation, so we jump ahead of time. We move before the cycle, we move while it's not economically advantageous. We don't buy low and sell high; we buy high and sell low. And we wonder why we have these losses. Now it takes tremendous astuteness, tremendous patience, and a gifted understanding of the laws of supply and demand to understand when in that cycle we should buy and when we should sell. So our question becomes, where do we enter that cycle? I would suggest timing is everything. Timing is critical and essential. Understand first and foremost the cycles of the business you are entering. Understand where you are in that cycle. I promise you all businesses will cycle eventually. Some will take three years, some will take ten years, but they will eventually cycle. And the person with the patience is usually the person who maximizes their return on investments. Whatever unit of measurement it is that determines success in your investment, it is usually the result of patience and timing in the cycle, and allowing the market, then, to come to you.

May I just say a word about family members in a family business. We have two very significant guidelines we have tried to teach our children from the time they were very small and in elementary school, that override all aspects of family businesses. Number one, cheer for your siblings. It is very difficult sometimes, but if they understand the importance of cheering for their siblings, great things can happen in a family business. The second critical guideline is the biblical expression we are all taught, which needs to be applied in the world of business as much as it does in the world of our religion. And that is simply to forgive and to forget. If one can apply those two simple characteristic guidelines—cheering for your siblings, and forgiving and forgetting and moving on in life—family businesses move from a negative to a remarkable positive. You simply cannot make it go unless you have the understanding and the attitude that the other person's success is your success. Thus, communication becomes

very essential in a family business. Whether it's a husband and
wife, whether it's a mother with one or two children, whether it's
a father and mother with many children, whether the business is
small, whether it's large, whether it's a five-person business or a
5,000- or 50,000-employee business, the basic rules are the same.
Communication must be effective and immediate. Letting problems fester will kill a family business quicker than anything else.

After communication in a family business, I would say let's
check our egos at the door. The demise of many family businesses result from egos that run unchecked. In a family business, more so than any other kind of business, we should never
use the word "I"; we should use the word "we." It is "we" and
it is "our." It is plural. We're a company of people. We are a
family of more than one. Let's give credit to others. It is such a
fundamental part of a family business. We must also realize that
in a family business, the common good benefits each individual.
Many family businesses keep several family members successful
and well, and in fulfillment of our needs, but first and foremost,
we must analyze in our family business, "Is this business successful for the common good of all of us?" And if we can stand
back and say, "Yes, this is helping all of us," then we have to say,
"I must place myself in a secondary position to the common
good of the business." This is something we learn at the feet
of our mothers and fathers at family nights. This is something
that can be taught when children are five and six and seven and
eight years old.

Our children become the products of our education. If we
are wise and prudent and educate our children in a way that

teaches them ethics, honor, decision making, and participation, that will be the kind of people they will become. I've always loved George Bernard Shaw, because he wrote that remarkable play *Pygmalion*, known in America as *My Fair Lady*. Little by little, Eliza became a princess, because she believed she was a princess, and she acted like she was a princess. She believed in every sense she would become one, and sure enough, she did. It's not just in fairy-tale land that this happens; it happens in family businesses, but it happens as a result of prudent mothers and fathers who take the time to train—and take the emotion, feeling, and passion of what they believe in—and allow their children to have a feeling, an understanding, and comprehension. Children are never too young. They understand much more than we think they do. They have such a sense of fun and they have no agenda and they sometimes can come back to us with answers that astound us. We have turned down more than one opportunity to buy or acquire major facilities because one of our children raised a question—a question you would have no idea they even knew existed.

At the end of the day, after we have built this business, it matters not too much what it is. What matters is that you have given it your full sense of emotion and feeling and passion, your full sense of integrity and honor, and a high degree of personal commitment. And then, when the book is finally written, we have to decide if we are successful, and success can vary enormously with the sizes of our businesses.

What do we owe back to society? What is it we need to repay that has permitted us to have this remarkable opportunity to go forward? Well, this is where the fun begins—in this great and remarkable capacity to put back into humankind some of what we have taken out. It's in a different format. What a joy it is to be able to borrow a little bit of the funding that goes on about us and to return that in a different format. I've thought many times how we would spend money if we had it. In the last few years, the Lord has blessed our business to be able to give considerable amounts to a number of causes. I never thought I would be in this position. I never deserved it, I never asked for it, and I never expected it. And yet, some way or another, the Lord has tapped me on the shoulder and said, "To you my son I am entrusting large amounts of money. You determine best how you can redeploy these assets into the community of humankind around you. You be the judge."

We receive thousands of letters a week. We have two full-time people who do nothing but answer requests for money. But over the years we have felt a great need to first and foremost focus on those who are suffering. Perhaps I spent too many years of my youth without outside plumbing, too many years with my mother going into a meat market after it closed to see if we could get some of the scraps. Perhaps I have observed over the years that those who are helping others, that those who can give back into society, even a small amount, are the happiest. I don't think the Lord will ever ask us, I don't think anyone will ever demand to know, "How much did you give?" I think the question would be better phrased, "Were you kind?" When President David O. McKay came to the Palo Alto, California area when I was a teenager, he said, "I'm going to tell you the most important secret of human life." I was sitting on the front row, and I watched President McKay as he said, "The most critical need of the human soul is to be kind." That's the greatest characteristic of mankind, and that's what the Savior wants us to do most.

I was watching television one night, 7 December 1988. I had come home from work, Karen and I had a bite to eat, flipped on the news about five minutes to ten, and saw a devastating earthquake in Armenia. I had never heard of Armenia. To me, it was just another country that started with an "A." A third of the country had been injured or killed. It was one of the worst natural disasters in the history of the twentieth century. The next morning I called a friend of mine, Dr. Armand Hammer in Los Angeles, and said, "Dr. Hammer, we must go to Armenia. They've had a devastating earthquake; they need us." Dr. Hammer had had excellent relationships with the Soviet Union throughout the Cold War. He had closer relationships than our own government did. He had been there many times. We quickly got on a plane and went over there. When I entered that country with our sons, and saw the devastation that had occurred, I said to the president of that land, "We will not leave until we have housed one hundred thousand people."

I didn't have the faintest idea what I was talking about. I didn't know how long it would take; I didn't know what it would cost. All I know is I felt impressed in my heart to tell the president of that country—a communist country at that time in 1989—I did not know how we would accomplish what I was committing to do, but I said, "We will provide." Over the last ten years, we've built the reinforced concrete for buildings now housing forty thousand people. I've told them we have another ten years left. I didn't know it would take twenty years. I didn't know it would take $50 million. I didn't know it would be a large part of my life. I didn't know our son Peter would go to Armenia twenty-six times. I didn't know we would be back and forth, that we would have operations there through the rest of my natural life. We have been through five different prime ministers and each one of them, as I have met them, has said, "Mr. Huntsman, everyone has left but you." And I said, "I gave my word. I told the prime minister and the president we would not leave until we had accomplished our objective. I had no idea how long that would take, but you're a remarkable people, you're a great land. We love your fighting spirit. We love to be part of this place." And so the stories go on forever about the enjoyment, the goodness, the experience, the excitement, and the thrill of giving.

I was in Jefferson County, Texas, about three weeks ago. We employ a lot of people in that part of the world, and I noticed a number of people there were getting cancer, and it bothered me. I told our people, "Meet with all of the hospitals, all eight of them in the county. I want every woman to be screened for breast cancer and every man for prostate cancer and we'll pay the total bill." I want the people of that county (there are about 350,000 of them) to know we love them, and that when we're there doing our business, we are there to take care of our fellow human beings, irrespective of race, religion, background, or ethnicity. It's very critical they understand our word is our bond, our love is their love, our interest is their interest, and our focus is their focus. Just this week, all the hospital switchboards have been jammed; all the doctors have been overly occupied. What a thrill it is because we will detect, early, hundreds of cases of people who have cancer, and we can save their lives.

Over the years, the homeless centers in different places have meant a lot to our family. Except for the grace of God, sometimes I wonder if we wouldn't be a recipient of their kindness and goodness. Over the years, we've spent a lot of money on homelessness and feeding the poor through different programs, mostly the Saint Vincent de Paul program of the Catholic Church, which our Church often uses. They're a wonderful program. We never know the people; we never meet the people; we'll never get to shake their hands. They'll never know our names; we'll probably never know their names. Our names will not be up in lights, we will not get to know them or understand them, but I received a letter recently from a lady. There was no return address. Inside all it said was Homeless Shelter. The letter said: "Dear Mr. Huntsman. I am warm and dry and out of the cold of last night, and I had a real bed to sleep on. I know you sent some money to keep this shelter, where I am staying, alive. I arose knowing I would shower with warm water and have soap and shampoo and a clean towel to use. Maybe this humble letter does not, or will not mean much within the vastness of the universe, but for this moment in time I just wanted to say with all my heart, thank you. For it means to me a great deal, to this homeless woman a great deal indeed. Thank you." I've had that letter framed, not because it's important to receive recognition for gifts, but because it's important to know the feelings in the hearts of people when they are down and out and receive help. And how grateful I am that she would take the time to send me that small token.

We will be dedicating the Huntsman Cancer Institute later this year. We are determined, someway, somehow, to find a cure for this dreaded disease. I've had prostate cancer and mouth cancer. My father died of prostate cancer. My mother died of breast cancer. Her father died of esophagus cancer. Cancer is in my mother's line very heavily. It is our hope and our prayer that someday these great researchers will find how to inoculate upon birth. To find out how to detect these tumors early will eliminate what happened to my dear friend Rex Lee, who served as president of this great institution. We hope, more than anything in the world, that in joining together with other major cancer research institutions, we can find a cure for this dreaded disease.

I was recently asked in New York if I would write a book, and it's kind of a flattering thing, I guess, but it was so unlikely and outrageous that anyone would ask that, that I kind of chuckled and said to the person, "You know, if I wrote a book, it would be the shortest book in the world. In fact, it would only be one page. In fact, it would only be one sentence. It would simply be entitled *Lucky, Lucky Me.* If anyone wanted to buy it they could feel free to buy it. But there isn't much I could say beyond that." That's how I feel.

ENDNOTE

1   TJ to Rogers and Slaughter, L&B. 11.92–93.

JON M. HUNTSMAN, SR.

One of Utah's most successful entrepreneurs, Jon Huntsman, Sr., is founder of the global Huntsman Chemical Corporation, the largest privately held chemical company in North America. The company oversees operations at thirty-eight sites around the globe, manufacturing more than four billion pounds of petrochemical products each year and employing more than five thousand people.

Huntsman is also widely known as one of America's foremost concerned citizens and philanthropists. He funded and developed the Huntsman Cancer Institute, a world-class research and treatment facility located on the University of Utah Campus in Salt Lake City.

He is the author of the book Winners Never Cheat: Everyday Values We Learned as Children (But May Have Forgotten).

Huntsman is a graduate of the Wharton School at the University of Pennsylvania, where he also earned his MBA.

This speech was given 19 June 1998 at the Fourth Annual BYU Management Conference.

ETHICAL PERFORMANCE IN THE PUBLIC SECTOR

by CAROLYN BOONE LEWIS

"The presence of trust with those we serve can be as important to success over time as the service we provide."

E thical performance of professional duties, exemplary moral conduct, a generous spirit, and personal traits that connect us, one to another, with kindness, integrity, and trust—these are qualities that I learned, subliminally, as a child, from parents who taught by precept and example. Along the way I've seen the value of being grounded in ethical principles, personally and professionally.

At the core of all that we are and all that we do is an ethical code—an internal compass—that registers our sense of right and wrong. It doesn't take much of a leap to get from the point of ethical behavior in one's personal life to a commitment to ethical performance in the public sector. They are rooted in the same principles; the same rules apply.

Beyond having the technical competence to perform, it is essential for the individual working in the public sector to have these personal traits:

1. set of personal values
2. moral underpinning
3. surefootedness about ethical responsibility
4. commitment to integrity and respect in relation to others
5. knowledge of the relevant legal and regulatory environment

Likewise, at the institutional level, experience has taught me the importance of building an ethical framework of organizational imperatives:

1. a statement of organizational values
2. a relevant, enforceable code of conduct
3. resources to support implementation
4. mechanisms for accountability
5. clarity about roles and relationships

A STATEMENT OF ORGANIZATIONAL VALUES

What values will guide the conduct of the business or service delivery of the organization? What standards apply? What can the public, consumer, or employee expect? Courtesy, respect, excellence, accountability? Whatever the values are, the rule is: "Make no assumptions." If we don't actively articulate and engage a set of organizational values, we start out with a deficit.

Engaging values requires being clear and explicit about how they apply to the daily activity in every phase of organizational life. The payoff is the building of trust and the creation of a yardstick by which all organizational behavior can be measured. The presence of trust with those we serve can be as important to success over time as the service we provide.

To put it differently, it's important to be intentional about the values we hold and to translate these values into the way we do business. Value-based decision making is a critical survival tool for organizations in times of crisis. In good and bad times, decision making that has a point of reference in well-articulated values builds morale and minimizes the background noise that gets in the way of excellence.

A RELEVANT, ENFORCEABLE CODE OF CONDUCT

A code is needed to draw the boundaries for acceptable behavior, to guide business practices and individual conduct, to help prevent conflicts of interest, and to foster a professional work environment. To be useful, the code must have relevance to the prevailing business environment. Perfunctory, boilerplate, "one-size-fits-all" language misses the point entirely.

At the Securities and Exchange Commission, where I spent years as a federal official in mutual fund regulation, a code of conduct for investment companies is required by statute. Boards of directors and investment advisors, who are in the business of managing assets held in trust for others, are in a fiduciary relationship with the investors. In general, such individuals are expected to act in the best interest of the company and its shareholders and not in a manner that uses inside information or the power of their position to inure to their personal benefit.

Translation: Act ethically. Violations can result in a range of sanctions, both civil and criminal.

In any area of public service, the cost of ethical transgressions, in dollars, reputation, and professional standing, can be considerable. Common sense is not viewed as enough of an antidote. As the American Hospital Association (AHA) has stressed in its Organizational Ethics Initiative, "It is clear that 'the ethical thing to do' cannot be taken for granted." It is also clear that the middle of a crisis is not the best time to start learning about ethical conduct and organizational integrity.

RESOURCES TO SUPPORT IMPLEMENTATION

Having a code of ethics, without resources to implement it, can sometimes be more deleterious than the absence of a policy. It's what I call the "fig leaf" trap. You think you're covered, but you aren't. In the implementation phase, it's important to engage the board, management, and staff at all levels in the process of determining the organizational ethics needs. Here, the leaders must set the tone.

When the board of trustees at Greater Southeast Healthcare System in Washington, D.C., where I have served as a board member for a number of years, took up the issue of organizational ethics, we emphasized the need for discrete staff resources, training (including training for the board), and mechanisms for integrating ethical values into the normal channels of decision making and other organizational activity. We also stressed the importance of having a mechanism for reporting, investigating, and correcting problems.

In organizations that make implementation a vital, visible process—that set a high-water mark for organizational integrity—there is a much better likelihood that the entire organization will behave ethically. As Somerset Maugham wrote: "It's a funny thing about life; if you refuse to accept anything but the best, you very often get it."

MECHANISMS FOR ACCOUNTABILITY

Values are the soul of an organization; a code of conduct, the teeth; resources for implementation, the arms and the legs. Now, for the heart of the matter—accountability.

It is important to have ongoing, systemic tools for accountability. The AHA's Organizational Ethics Initiative notes, "A commitment to a sustained ethical environment can be a direct force in heightening the excellence, efficiency, productivity, and morale of any health care organization. A strong organizational ethics foundation will help resolve conflicts within and between professional groups."

The same holds true for the public sector. My minister, the Reverend Canon Dalton Downs, often reminds us, "In the final analysis, religion is not about what you believe. It is about what you do." So it is with ethical performance.

A strong component of accountability is embodied in maintaining openness in the performance of public service. A credible process for accountability—one that has integrity—is an important tool. Remember, the management of public service resources is everybody's business. Justice Louis D. Brandeis said, "Sunshine is the best disinfectant."

Two other key components of accountability are: 1) providing a process where everyone in the organization can speak out without fear of reprisal (the airline industry calls this a "blame free" environment), and 2) demonstrating commitment to ethical behavior from all components of the organization, especially top management. Reducing ethics in an organization to a committee function undermines accountability. Ethical transgressions are rooted in individual behavior and flourish in an environment of organizational inattention. A committee can certainly help, but not if it is seen as the locus of organizational ethics, or the "ethics cop."

CLARITY ABOUT ROLES AND RELATIONSHIPS

Creating an ethical environment requires clarity about roles, relationships, and lines of responsibility. Leadership style, organizational culture, the day-to-day demands of the workplace—all can foster informal lines of reporting and create gaps in accountability. A clearly articulated organizational framework can be a helpful mechanism for maintaining accountability and trust.

Five personal traits and five organizational imperatives—closely linked and interdependent. The coming together of the two, ethical personal behavior and organizational integrity, creates an environment where challenges to ethical performance in the workplace can be dealt with rationally, fairly, and effectively. The challenges can be highly visible, such as those dealing with conflicts of interest in procurement and the awarding of contracts or generous bonuses and severance packages for senior management (the latter often seen as rewards for lackluster performance). They can also be less transparent, for example, taking shortcuts in a process to keep productivity up or providing public information that falls short of full disclosure. In this high-tech, information-rich age, new ethical challenges will overwhelm us. We face issues such as balancing a respect for privacy with the public's right to know; designing performance measurements that respect and reflect the growing cultural and ethnic diversity in the workplace; and treating employees fairly and the public/community interest equitably in mergers and consolidations.

To cloud the picture even more, ethical decisions are often about organizational conflicts between competing, legitimate initiatives. In health care, these conflicts raise ethical considerations of the most complex nature, for example: What kind of care should be provided at the end of life? Should the hospital merge and risk losing its community identity, stand alone and risk going under, or close?

This takes us back to values. A system of ethics provides values and principles by which we make decisions and creates a climate where ethical decisions are natural and expected.

We are in a period of tentative, hence declining, commitment to ethical behavior. It's what I call "on the other hand" behavior. It's about knowing what's called for, knowing the right thing to do, or, at the very least, seeing the caution light that says "go slow—danger ahead," but saying to yourself, circumstances being what they are: "the demands of the moment are so pressing; I have a deadline to meet; competition is too fierce—we will lose market share; the ends justify the means; or, that slippery slope—just this one time . . . ." You get the picture. "I know I'm on soft ground, but on the other hand . . . ."

The fact is, we do have to make choices—every one of us, every day. In my view, professional acumen plus ethical leadership is the most effective agent for noble public service.

In an article entitled "Ethically Speaking," ethical behavior is defined as "acting with integrity, honesty, competence, respect, fairness, trust, courage, and responsibility."[1] A tall order. If it is true that the devil is in the details, I would suggest that the angels are on the side of working through the complexities with a very simple determination to do the right thing and to design systems and workplaces that support those efforts.

Ethical performance is, at once, a compact with oneself and a commitment to others to always do the right thing. Mark Twain said, "Always do right. This will surprise some people and astonish the rest."

On a more serious note, ethical performance challenges us to set our moral compass and stay the course, missteps and mistakes notwithstanding. In the words of a Hindu proverb, "There is nothing noble in being superior to some other man. The true nobility is being superior to your previous self."

ENDNOTE

1   P. Haddock and M. Manning, (1990, March). "Ethically speaking." *Sky*, pp. 128–131.

CAROLYN BOONE LEWIS

Carolyn Boone Lewis was president of the CBL Group and chair-elect of the American Hospital Association. She worked for more than twenty years as a senior government official and was a recognized leader in major national and local organizations, both in the public and private sectors. Lewis demonstrated her expertise in the areas of finance, investment management, business and organizational development, and health care by shaping and directing organizational growth, corporate restructuring, developing policy, and creating consensus with people from diverse backgrounds.

Her professional experience included serving as assistant director of the division of investment management for the United States Securities and Exchange Commission and serving as one of five national board members for the United States Department of Health and Human Services. Her volunteerism extended to the national Forum of Women Health Care Leaders, Chicago; the Mayor's Health Policy Council, Washington, D.C.; and the Joint Commission on the Accreditation of Health Care Organizations. She received the Tribute of Excellence Award and the Distinguished Service Award from the District of Columbia Hospital Association for her community service.

Lewis graduated magna cum laude *with a BS in accountancy from Hampton University in Virginia and completed graduate studies in finance at George Washington University.*

She delivered this address in 1998, when she was honored as the Administrator of the Year by the Marriott School's Romney Institute of Public Management.

PERSONAL LEADERSHIP AND PERSONAL CHARACTER

by JOHN E. PEPPER

> *"Integrity manifests itself in a quality*
> *I have come to appreciate more and more:*
> *'authenticity.'"*

t is really quite an honor and thrill to be with you at Brigham Young University today. This is the first time that I've been on your campus. Yours is a university, however, with which I've long been familiar, for several reasons. Not least, your football team. Also, the association with the university by Stephen Covey, who has had quite an impact in my own life and that of many in my company, and particularly I think of Brigham Young University because of your alumni who've made such good contributions to Procter & Gamble.

It's fair to say that my knowledge and respect for this institution deepened enormously in the past month because I have come to understand your mission far better preparing for my visit today. It is truly a noble mission—one I resonate to tremendously.

My comments today will, in many ways, deal with how I and my company try to live a very similar mission. My comments will deal with two tightly linked subjects: personal leadership and the role of personal character in forging strong leadership.

I am often asked, "What is the most important thing you have learned in your career?" My answer is simple and immediate: "Personal leadership makes things happen." I have seen the power of personal leadership in many venues.

I have seen the difference that Procter & Gamble leaders make in running more than seventy country operations and dozens of product line operations. I have seen the difference that individual principals make in more than seventy-five public schools and that individual teachers make in thousands of classrooms in Cincinnati.

What defines great leadership? What does great leadership entail? It has many dimensions, of course. The mission of leadership, it seems to me, is to guide and enable purposeful growth of individuals and institutions. It is to create and sustain a purposeful future. Growth is both an imperative and a noble pursuit for many reasons. Not only does it contrast to the only ultimate alternative-decline—but creates value for stakeholders, whether they be shareholders of a company or students on a campus. Purposeful growth also creates a sense of pride and excitement for employees because they are part of a winning team—and it is no wonder that is what attracts the best talent. Never has it been so important for leaders to deliver on their mission of growth and creating the future, for never have the opportunities been so great, at least in our business.

That is a result of the explosion of digital technology and globalization.

I have found the attributes of intelligence, imagination, personal sensitivity, energy, and strategic focus to be essential. At Procter & Gamble, we have found it useful to focus on three components of personal leadership. We call them the three Es: envisioning, energizing, and enabling. Rather than talking about these elements, however, I thought I would talk with you tonight on a more personal level about what I have come to believe is the most defining characteristic of the most effective leaders I have known. That is personal character. What is character? I don't know if there is a final answer, but for me character begins with integrity: "Being as one." "Being as one" in the sense of being faithful in action to your most important core values, to your promises, to your words. "Being as one" in saying what you mean and meaning what you say, and of being faithful to other people, especially when they are not present.

Integrity manifests itself in a quality I have come to appreciate more and more: "authenticity." I love to hear it said of someone: "What you see is what you get." No matter where this person is, no matter who they are talking with, they are the same because they are just being themselves. They operate from a hard inner core of values and beliefs. It is easy to think of heroic, authentic figures. Vaclav Havel risking his life denouncing communism from a prison cell in Czechoslovakia. Nelson Mandela doing the same about apartheid in South Africa. Senator John McCain unyielding thirty years ago to his captors in a Vietnamese prison camp; more recently in Cincinnati denouncing large campaign contributions right in front of some of his very biggest potential contributors.

However, this need for character—for integrity and authenticity—isn't a sometimes thing. It arises every day in the workplace in Procter & Gamble, in my associations with my family, and among all of you right here at Brigham Young University. It is one thing to describe character as being faithful to one's values; it is another to ask, "What is good character?"

I have tried to answer that by trying to answer another question, which I am sure each of you have raised, "How, when all is said and done, does one measure the value of a life? What, really, should leave a person feeling good inside, with lasting joy and satisfaction?"

I recorded my own convictions on this long ago. They are very simple. First, try to be all I can be. To the best of my ability, try to serve my highest instincts and reach my full potential, leading and persisting in what I believe to be most important.

Second, in doing this, trying to be of service to others. But how does one go about this? Personally, I don't think anything is as important as having a clear sense of values and purpose. I believe that values really do determine your approach to life, in everything you do.

I like what Margaret Thatcher once said: "You must start with beliefs. Yes, always with beliefs. You first sort out what you believe in. You then apply it. You don't compromise things that matter." She added, "It is not enough to be a starter. You have to be a sticker and see it through." How true!

Of course, your values have to be put to work against a particular purpose, and they need to be something you believe in deeply. Every person I have seen who has been successful has had that one thing in common. They have been very clear and very passionate about what they are doing, about its value. And it has been a purpose they honestly believe to be worthy of their best efforts.

From Michael Jordan to Sam Walton to Martin Luther King, Jr., from the professors here at BYU who you'll never forget, to the men and women at Procter & Gamble who I have seen make the biggest contributions, they all have one quality in common: they care deeply about what they are doing, and they are committed to doing it very, very well.

All of you here tonight have already experienced this. Reflect for just a brief moment, if you will, on your biggest successes, those accomplishments you are most proud of in your studies or in a sport or an extracurricular activity. Whatever it is, I'll bet it is an activity that you really love and have devoted yourself to most completely.

As you go ahead to the next stage of your life after college, it will be no different. You may not find it in your first job. It may not come out and grab you, but look for it. Find an activity that you love to do and make sure it is part of an institution or career whose values are a good match with your own.

I found this at Procter & Gamble, and it changed my life. For what I found is that the purpose and values of this company and its people were very much in accord with my own. What's more, I have found that they helped strengthen my own values and bring them to life.

Indeed, I can tell you that of all the reasons I am still with Procter & Gamble after thirty-six years, the most important are the people and values of this place. And that brings me to a point that I think should be very encouraging to you. I have found that the values of a company are a huge determinant of its success.

By that I mean that pursuing strong corporate values is not only the right thing to do ethically, but it is also the best way to build a winning leadership business. There are several reasons why this is true.

First of all, a company's values have everything to do with who is attracted to your company, and, even more, who will stay with it. Each of us has only one life to live. We want to live it in a career committed to high goals and high-sighted means of reaching those goals. This is true everywhere I have ever been—in our most mature countries and in emerging industrialists, like China and eastern Europe.

Beyond that, strong corporate values greatly simplify decision-making. I can't overemphasize how liberating it really is to know the things you won't even have to think about doing. You don't waste time even in talking about them. About diluting a product. Or taking a bribe. What's more, strong values earn the respect of customers and suppliers and governments and other companies, too. This is absolutely crucial in the long term. Finally, strong values in a company create trust and pride among its employees. They build the morale, the spirit of the place. And that produces better results.

Now, just as is the case with each of us personally, values in a company aren't worth the paper they are printed on unless they are reflected in actions and decisions, especially the tough calls between the expedient and the principled, between what's right for the short and long term. We often face such calls in our business. Many occur in the way we treat our consumers. Nowhere is that more important than product safety, but even in this area the decision can be less clear-cut than you might think. If you know a product is unsafe for some reason, you pull it off the market. No decision could be easier.

But what if you can't be sure that your product is unsafe? What if you even believe that it is safe, yet you can't prove it categorically? What do you do then? How do you justify what can be a very expensive decision? There is no single answer, unfortunately, that applies to every situation like this. You simply have to depend on your judgment and do what you believe is the right thing.

An example from our experience was our decision to withdraw our Rely Feminine Protection product in the 1970s. Since science did not allow us to separate categorically the disease of toxic shock syndrome from product attributes in that category, we closed down the brand. There was not then, nor is there now, evidence that we were directly involved, but we refused to take the chance. In today's terms, that decision cost us hundreds of millions of dollars. But in our judgment, based on our values, it was the right thing to do.

We faced another, truly bizarre situation more recently. Counterfeiters started to produce and distribute a fake Head & Shoulders product. We found that, in a rare case, use of the fake, poorly made product might cause severe illness. What should we do? After all, it wasn't even our product. Well, what we did do was advertise in newspapers to advise people who might buy this counterfeit product not to use it. Here we were, trying to protect consumers from a product we had not even made—but clearly the right thing to do.

Another situation we sometimes face is how to deal with sensitive information about a competitor. Here's a real-life example. A senior executive from one of our advertising agencies got into a cab in New York and found a computer disk lying on the floorboard that included the marketing plans from one of our toughest competitors. If that had happened to you, what would you have done with the disk? What would you have expected someone who worked for you, an employee or a supplier, to do with that disk?

I am pleased to say that in this case the agency executive sent the disk back to the chairman of the competitive company, assuring him that neither the agency nor anyone at Procter had looked at the contents of the disk. As his letter said, "We always compete with commitment and intensity, but we'll never compromise our ethics to win."

Another situation that arises in our business that tests our values is a request for improper payment, a bribe. For example, a couple of years ago we had a shipment of material needed to produce Pampers diapers worth about a quarter of a million dollars arrive at a country in western Africa. We knew its import was allowed, but the customs inspector pretended that this material fell under classification that forbids its import, quickly adding that he was willing to release the shipment if we gave him $5,000 under the table. What do you do? In the scheme of things, $5,000 isn't that much money. Is it worth $5,000 to move a quarter million dollars worth of raw materials? To keep a line operating? To avoid having to explain to your boss that you let a multimillion-dollar business be disrupted over $5,000?

What I can tell you is that our division manager in charge refused to even contemplate any such discussion. In fact, the material remained blocked. We had to shut down our plant for four months. We had to write letters and seek government interventions all the way up to the president of the country to get our materials cleared legally. But we finally did it. There is no question that the cost of our business far exceeded what it would have taken to just pay the bribe. Many local people thought we were crazy or naive for choosing the course we did, but that didn't sway us. They may think we didn't know how to do business, but they will respect our integrity.

One of the central values at Procter & Gamble is the appropriateness of our supporting communities in which we live and work. And happily, once again I have found that to not only be the "right thing to do" but also to be right for our business. Why? Well, first of all, I have found that companies with a genuine community commitment attract strong employees who have that same kind of commitment. Second, these companies also earn the respect of local communities and local governments. That can be very helpful in gaining appropriate support on important business issues. What's more, we need the leadership of men and women from business if we are to have the kind of communities that our businesses and employees need. We are not going to improve many of the institutions we depend on—education, government, the arts—without leadership from men and women who have the knowledge and competitive toughness acquired in business. Finally, involvement in community activities also helps develop one's own personal capabilities. For example, I trace my own appreciation of the power of diversity directly to my work in the community, from interacting with people of great talent and spirit from different backgrounds. I would not be the person I am today without this experience.

So, the pursuit of sound values is not only the right thing to do ethically, but it is also critical to business success. But how does one develop and live such values? Well, that takes me right back to the subject of personal character. The longer I have lived, the more I have come to realize that developing and living the character I seek is my ultimate personal challenge.

There are three watchwords I've tried to keep constantly in front of me as I've pursued this challenge. They are wisdom, courage, and persistence. Wisdom to identify the right things to do—to distinguish between those things I can and should change, and those I cannot and should not change. Wisdom to decide what is the right balance between the short and long term. Courage to put aside the fear of failure, recognizing that if I am to accomplish anything of real value, I must risk wrong decisions. Courage to fight for what I believe in, especially if it is controversial, not letting the views of others deter me from something I believe in deeply. Courage in following my deepest instincts, even if the future is not clear.

I'll always remember what a speaker said about that at my oldest son's graduation: "Sometimes you have to leap before you look." That's right. "Leap before you look." I know that feeling, and you probably do, too. Embarking on something that you are not sure you can do, but being sure it is right and that you need to try. I have found many of the most important things in life are like that. The very promising organizational change that we are embarked on now at Procter & Gamble has been like that for me. When we started, I was not sure where it would lead. And I didn't know exactly what my role would be. But I was absolutely convinced it was right to do for the future of the company. And so I went ahead.

When I helped launch the Cincinnati Youth Collaborative in 1987, I did not know exactly what we should do, but I felt sure that we needed to pull together a group of people from different parts of the community to work on behalf of our youth. So we set off to do it. When I agreed to cochair the fund-raising campaign for the new National Underground Railroad Freedom Center that will be located in Cincinnati, I didn't know—indeed, I still don't know—exactly how we're going to raise the required $90 million. But I believed deeply that this is an undertaking that is needed, and I felt that I should help make it happen.

Success on this, I am sure, will require a good dose of the third watchword I mentioned: persistence. I can't overemphasize the importance of sheer persistence to success. History is written largely with the significance of persistence—but it is written in invisible ink. History records the happy endings and glosses over the failures along the way. But they were there. You can be sure of that. On almost anything of real importance, success has only been achieved because some man or woman had the grit to keep going.

You probably have all heard the story about one of our most famous presidents. A man who ran a country store early in his life but went broke and took fifteen years to pay off the debt. He got married, but had an unhappy marriage. He ran for the House of Representatives but lost—not once, but twice. So what did he do next? He ran for the Senate—again, not once, but twice—and again, he lost twice. Attacked daily by the press, despised by half the country, that catalog of disappointments would have driven most people to despair. Not this man. His name was Abraham Lincoln.

I am sure all of you could tell me who made the first manned flight—the Wright brothers at Kitty Hawk, North Carolina, in 1903. Of course. But could you tell me how many times the Wright brothers had tried, unsuccessfully, to fly their plane before the success we read about? Five times? Ten times? Fifty times? No, they had attempted this flight more than one hundred times. And each time, they failed. But they didn't give up. The importance of persistence is especially vital today in business because in the world-class competition around us, the margin between success and failure is usually very slim indeed.

Norm Augustine, a member of our board of directors, tells an interesting story about the Iditarod dogsled race in northern Alaska. It takes place over 1,048 miles of inhospitable terrain. The contestants encounter winds of up to one hundred miles per hour, temperatures down to seventy degrees below zero. But the incredible thing, from the standpoint of persistence, is that in one recent race the person who finished second lost the grueling sixteen-day race by a mere one second.

Wisdom, courage, persistence. Qualities that, in my experience, underpin strong personal character. Now, it will not come as news to you to hear me say that it is far easier to describe the qualities of strong character than to live them. And, I thought I would share some of the things I personally have found to be most helpful, and most challenging in this respect.

First on the helpful side: I have gained great benefit, I believe, from writing down and updating at least annually what I view as my core responsibilities and opportunities to contribute and improve. I have done this for at least twenty years. Second, I have been greatly helped by reading outstanding authors— some old, like Thoreau and the Bible; and some new, like John Gardner, Stephen Covey, and John Kotter. I continue to learn. Third, I have benefited tremendously from the outstanding people I have come to know over the years. I have learned from and been strengthened by working with Procter & Gamble people. People in the community. People with vocations to service. And I have been strengthened by my wife and children. Never forget, your personal associations really do matter. Finally, the longer I live the more I learn the importance of the consistency with which I practice good values. It sure doesn't make it easy, but I have found that each violation of what I believe is right, even if it isn't the biggest deal in the world, is a crack.

Ronald Reagan had it right in the talk he gave in 1993: "The character that takes command in moments of crucial choices has already been determined by a thousand other choices made earlier at seemingly unimportant moments. It has been determined by all of the seemingly little choices of years past, by all those times when the voice of conscience was at war with the voice of temptation, whispering, aloud or internal, 'It doesn't really matter.'"

President Reagan's comments remind me of another story told by Norm Augustine. Norm dramatized the importance of trying to do what is right—consistently, constantly—by examining the habits of, of all things, a snake: the boa constrictor. Norm once felt, as I did, that the boa made its kill by quickly crushing its victim in the powerful folds of its body. However, his look in the encyclopedia revealed instead that the boa places two or three coils of its body around the chest of its prey and each time the victim exhales its breath, the boa simply takes up the slack. After three or four breaths, there is no more slack. The prey quickly suffocates and is then swallowed by the boa.

Norm went on to note, rather chillingly, that this deadly phenomenon of the victim becoming an unwitting accomplice in its own destruction is not confined to the world of reptiles. The boa we have to face and overcome is following our ethical values—each lapse is another coil of the snake.

Still, I have to offer a strong caution here. We must not be too hard on ourselves. Try as we might, no one of us will ever be perfect—not even close to perfect—in living up to our highest ideals. So we have to strike a balance here. Complacency and weak-willed indifference are like quicksand. But we must realize that to err is human. It will happen. I think the key is to go on with more determination, recognizing that the consistency with which we act in line with our best instincts will give us greater confidence and greater strength for the future.

Trying to do this, I certainly have faced challenges in living the character I want. One has been the challenge of establishing clear and honest expectations in my relationships with others, particularly in confronting disagreements that involve a lot of tension. Sometimes, I have been too reluctant to do this. More and more I have seen the need to get key issues on the table, sooner rather than later. Relationship problems are not like wine—they don't get better with age. I also have suffered sometimes from the inevitable tendency to postpone what comes the hardest. I say that even as I have tried to keep the maxim of "doing first things first" front and center.

Finally, I believe I could have engaged more often and earlier on really new experiences. As you might imagine, I have done a lot of this. But, in hindsight, I could have done even more. In that regard, I would emphasize how experiential learning has been the most important learning for me—throwing myself into different situations, especially those in which I feel uncomfortable. I have found that this willingness to embark on new experiences, often uncertain, sometimes uncomfortable, and even a bit frightening, is key to growth. That has become clear and clearer to me as the years have gone by.

I am going to conclude by addressing a question that I have been asked many times: "How do you think ethics and values tie corporate, public, and private lives together?"

The answer is that they should do it superbly. I believe it is perilous to have different sets of values for different parts of your life. I don't think you can compartmentalize these things. I know that my effectiveness and my peace of mind demand that the values that guide my life in Procter & Gamble, in community activities, in my family life, and in the privacy of my own mind and heart be as much the same as possible. For me, those values come down to five things:

PASSION: believing deeply in and loving what I do.

AUTHENTICITY: being myself as well as I personally can.

TRUTH: pursuing it at all costs, no matter where it leads.

ENTHUSIASM: realizing that nothing great happens without it.

RESPECT AND CARING FOR OTHERS: deep-seated caring, evidenced in what you do.

These qualities of leadership and character become real, of course, only as we live them to the best of our ability in our actions and decisions every day. If my life is any example, doing this will not produce a life free from tension or free from frustrations stemming from actions that too often fall short of our ideals. But in the end, it will produce a life filled with a good measure of personal satisfaction, growth, joy, and contribution. And, in the words of that famous song, "Who could ask for anything more?"

Yes, personal leadership makes things happen, and strong personal character, forged in the daily encounters of challenge and opportunity, is the ultimate key to that leadership.

JOHN E. PEPPER

John Pepper is a "leader of exceptional distinction . . . who has long been regarded as one of the nation's most principled and successful business leaders," said Yale President Richard C. Levin in January 2004 as he announced Pepper's appointment as vice president for finance and administration at Yale University.

Pepper retired in 2002 as chairman of the board of Procter & Gamble, where he devoted thirty-nine years creating and leading one of the world's largest consumer products companies. During his tenure as president and CEO, Procter & Gamble was regularly cited by Fortune magazine as one of America's "Most Admired Companies."

Pepper has also been a key force in the creation of the Cincinnati Youth Collaborative and the National Underground Railroad Freedom Center. He is director of Boston Scientific and formerly on the boards of Xerox Corporation and Motorola, Inc. He also served as chairman of the U.S. Advisory Committee for Trade Policy and Negotiations.

Pepper graduated from Yale University in 1960 and holds honorary doctorate degrees from Xavier University, Mount St. Joseph College, Ohio State University, and St. Petersburg University (Russia).

This address was given at BYU's Marriott School when Pepper received the International Executive of the Year Award 29 October 1999.

MOTIVATORS IN BUSINESS

by L. ALDIN PORTER

*"Rarely have I seen
one who is highly motivated by excellence
fall prey to the disease of pride or greed."*

I am honored to speak to you tonight. You are a very select group whose contributions in the years ahead will be monumental. I know many of those who will be your teachers and your mentors. You are not likely to understand tonight what a rare group they are. You will be marvelously blessed through their efforts.

As you can see, I am getting along in years, and old men love to give advice to young people. But be careful. I have learned that free advice often costs more than the kind you pay for. Tonight, I would like to visit and share some concepts I wish I had known or at least been reminded of at your age. I also want to raise a voice of warning to those of you who will make business your lifelong work.

I have been honored to be a General Authority these past fourteen years. But today would like to focus on the nearly thirty years I spent working in the business world. During my career, I learned that four things generally motivate people in business. If you will consider these four sources of motivation, you will have additional criteria to consider when planning a course of action for yourselves and, eventually, for those you supervise.

MONEY

It is understandable that money is motivating. It is appropriate that you expend great effort in earning it. Money will permit you to raise a family and also to make substantial contributions to the Church and to other worthy causes. But this desire must be controlled. When we are motivated by money, we can let it explode into greed. At one point in my life, I realized that I was constantly going into the counting house to see how much money I had made that week or even that day. Beware!

Mormon understood the results of this problem. "And the people began to be distinguished by ranks, according to their riches and their chances for learning; yea, some were ignorant because of their poverty, and others did receive great learning because of their riches."[1] Note also that Mormon precedes this statement with, "For there were many merchants in the land, and also many lawyers, and many officers." [2]

It appears that merchants have some part in people being distinguished by ranks. If you are not motivated by greed, the day will come when additional money will lose part of its powerful motivating force in your life.

COMPETITION

Often, money and competition march together. It is healthy to compete. It can be a positive motivator and a major factor in helping achieve goals. But it can also harden us and blind us to the needs of others.

The day will come when you will have earned the respect of your peers and won enough competitions that this factor will lose much of its appeal. Control the desire to be seen as the best. Striving to be *seen* rather than striving to *be* is dangerous. I have observed as much dishonesty caused by a desire to be seen as number one as I have seen caused by a desire for money. Either one can cause you to make decisions that will later bring you a great deal of regret.

If you prove successful in obtaining money and receiving the plaudits of men, beware of pride. I draw your attention to counsel given by President Ezra Taft Benson. He said: "The proud make every man their adversary by pitting their intellects, opinions, works, wealth, talents, or any other worldly measuring device against others." C. S. Lewis wrote in his book *Mere Christianity:* "Pride gets no pleasure out of having something, only out of having more of it than the next man."

A DESIRE FOR EXCELLENCE

A desire for excellence is different than a desire to win awards for excellence. That falls under competition. This objective is not for anyone else, not for money, and not for fame. It is to rise to a benchmark set by you and only you—an internal standard that is one's own acceptable level of performance. This motivator will keep you up at night when your peers, supervisor, and president of the company are happily asleep. This level of maturity separates the majority of mankind from the few. Rarely have I seen one who is highly motivated by excellence fall prey to the disease of pride or greed.

BELIEF IN A CAUSE

This becomes a strong motivating factor when you no longer are the primary focus. This moves people when they see a larger purpose than their own. This higher level of motivation is quite common to parents, missionaries, and priesthood and auxiliary leaders. In fact, it is very common in the Church and quite rare in the business world.

Abigail Adams, as reported in David McCullough's outstanding biography on John Adams, said: "Posterity who are to reap the blessings will scarcely be able to conceive the hardships and sufferings of their ancestors."[3] Note the sacrifice was being made by those who would not likely "reap the blessings."

When you are willing to make considerable sacrifices for posterity or anyone besides yourself, you are on the brink of finding a cause. On one occasion I was in the East having breakfast with a very prominent man in the financial planning world. I had played a small part in a presentation he was preparing—a retirement plan for several thousand employees of a major corporation. He told me of the hours into the night he had worked on the presentation. I looked at him for a long time and said, "You have more money than you or your children can possibly spend. You are recognized in the entire industry as a man of superior talents. You have received all of the major awards. Why would you work so hard and so long on this project?"

His response indicated what I am trying to convey. He said: "I am plagued by the knowledge that if I don't do my work well, someone will suffer." His primary concern was not about the senior officers of the company. They would not suffer. He was greatly concerned about the rest of the people in that organization.

Those are the four powerful motivating factors of the business world. Other factors that fall into additional categories are also helpful to discuss.

LEARN TO HANDLE MONEY AS A TOOL

Money is the means by which you can accomplish important things. A hammer is a tool. If one learns to use it well, a house can be built. If one doesn't use it well there will be many broken and bruised and very painful thumbs.

Let me explain. Assume your income is $50,000 a year. Your outgo is $52,000. Eventually you will find yourself in slavery. Your creditors will own you. If your income is $50,000 and your outgo is $48,000, you will almost certainly live in a world of freedom. You will control the tool of money. Money is a tool—use it wisely.

When I returned as a young man from my mission, I reported to Elder LeGrand Richards. He gave me counsel on very practical matters. One was to pay tithing. He said: "Save an equal amount." Invest it first in education for you and your spouse. Second, invest in a home. Third, invest wherever you think wise. But be more concerned about the return *of* your money than the return *on* your money.

President Gordon B. Hinckley in October 1998 Priesthood Session of General Conference said:

"So many of our people are living on the very edge of their incomes. In fact, some are living on borrowings. We have witnessed in recent weeks wide and fearsome swings in the markets of the world. The economy is a fragile thing. A stumble in the economy in Jakarta or Moscow can immediately affect the entire world. It can eventually reach down to each of us as individuals. There is a portent of stormy weather ahead to which we had better give heed."

Might I say that those words are filled with warning from one who is a seer, one who can see afar off and through his prophetic insight raise a warning voice. Here is one counseling us who is immersed in a cause.

President Hinckley continued:

"I am troubled by the huge consumer installment debt which hangs over the people of the nation, including our own people. I recognize that it may be necessary to borrow to get a home, of course. But let us buy a home that we can afford and thus ease the payments which will constantly hang over our heads without mercy or respite for as long as thirty years.

I urge you, brethren, to look to the condition of your finances. I urge you to be modest in your expenditures; discipline yourselves in your purchases to avoid debt to the extent possible. Pay off debt as quickly as you can, and free yourselves from bondage.

This is a part of the temporal gospel in which we believe. May the Lord bless you, my beloved brethren, to set your houses in order."[4]

KNOW WHAT YOU STAND FOR

You should know by now what you stand for and where you draw the line. Permit me an example. A young man graduated from the University of Idaho in business at the top of his class. He received a job with a major corporation in the East. He and his wife traveled to their new location with much excitement and enthusiasm. He was to begin on a Monday morning. When they and other trainees arrived, they were invited to a get-acquainted party Sunday evening at the president's home. There were cocktails, inappropriate language, and stories that were embarrassing to both husband and wife. They talked about it that night and decided they would live the commandments and be courteous and patient. The next morning the young man was invited into the personnel officer's suite and told by him that he would not be happy there. He said, "You just don't fit in." The young couple was crushed. They couldn't believe it.

They came to see me. I had been his stake president during his high school days. They felt the Lord had let them down. "If you feel that way, why didn't you agree to drink and participate?" "Because that would be wrong." "Well, you had a choice. You could have denied what you believe to be true and kept the job or have stood by your convictions and lost the job. What should it have been?" They answered: "We did the right thing." "Of course you did."

Decide early in your life where you stand. It will save a lot of time and energy in the future. Keep your covenants. Be worthy of help from unseen sources. I can assure you that many times when you are under stress you will receive helpful impressions. One statement the Lord made has helped me many times when I did not know how to escape a problem: "All flesh is in mine hands; be still and know that I am God."[5]

HUMILITY AND RECOGNITION OF OTHERS

Kathryn Graham, the owner and publisher of the *Washington Post*, invited Ronald and Nancy Reagan to her home near the end of President Reagan's administration. There were about six hundred people in attendance. There was an accident, and a glass and its contents fell to the carpet. Graham came on the scene, and recalls, "I was dumbstruck at seeing the president of the United States on his hands and knees in the middle of the crowd picking up the ice." On the phone the next day Nancy Reagan told Graham of the time the president was in the hospital after the assassination attempt. The president was not to be out of his bed, but he got up and went to the bathroom. In the process he spilled a pitcher of water. When the attendants came in, he was on his hands and knees wiping it up. When Nancy asked him why, he said that he was afraid the nurse would get into trouble.[6]

Remember others—most of you will achieve much in your life—be humble. And be aware of the contribution others will make to your success. Understand that you aren't likely to accomplish much in this world alone—not in business—certainly not in family, not in church, and almost never in anything that will bring you happiness. Always remember others who helped you succeed.

YOUR SPOUSE—THE MOST IMPORTANT FACTOR OF ALL

Decide with your spouse what it is you really want in life. What do you want to leave behind when your work here is finished? Think lifelong. What I am going to say may not be politically correct, but I believe it to be true nevertheless.

A good marriage has a division of labor. After deciding your lifetime objective, decide how the two of you will divide the work to achieve it. For example, a superb executive secretary could be paid as much as $50 an hour. But the same person may be a superb writer—understandable, graphic, and clear. That person might be paid as much as $100 an hour or more. What should that person do with his or her talent? Wisdom would dictate that he or she should put the talent to the highest and best use.

Please forgive me for a personal example. Sister Porter graduated from the University of Houston with a degree in accounting about the time she turned twenty. She learned to run large banking machines then in use in major banks. This was at the time the computer was just being developed. She then became an instructress for Burroughs Adding Machine Company. When Burroughs would sell a machine, she would go into a bank for several weeks and teach others how to use it. She was, for that era, highly paid.

She could earn considerably more money than I could even after I graduated from BYU. I was a sophomore at BYU when we were married. We decided we would not put off having a family. Shirley worked until it was time to quit when she was expecting our first child. The return on having her at home was far greater in contributing toward our objectives than if she had continued to work outside the home.

Our six children had a mother—a full-time mother. You cannot imagine the impact that has had on our happiness in life. Without a doubt she has done that which has brought the greatest return to us. In addition, her contribution to my capacity to earn an income is beyond calculation. Our family has brought us many times more joy and happiness than any worldly recognition or wealth could.

Let me close by saluting you for your decision to continue to prepare yourselves. You will leave here well educated and go out into the world. You must be men and women of integrity who will spread wide the principles of this institution and of the kingdom of God. That you may do so is my prayer.

ENDNOTES

1   3 Nephi 6:12.
2   3 Nephi 6:11.
3   David McCullough, *John Adams*, 169.
4   Gordon B. Hinckley, "To the Boys and to the Men," *Ensign*, Nov. 1998, 54.
5   Doctrine and Covenants 101:16.
6   Kathryn Graham, *Personal History*, 612.

L. ALDIN PORTER

Aldin Porter is former Senior President of the Seventy of The Church of Jesus Christ of Latter-day Saints. For nearly thirty years, Elder

Porter was affiliated with Mutual of New York. He is past president of the Idaho chapter of Certified Life Underwriters and has been president of the Utah Real Estate Planning Council. He is a member of the board of directors of the Beneficial Financial Group.

He gave this speech at the BYU Marriott School graduate student orientation 31 August 2001.

RULES OF BUSINESS, LAWS OF GOD: THE SEARCH FOR ETHICS IN BUSINESS

by KEVIN B. ROLLINS

"Realizing our potential as individuals,
as a company, and as a society,
requires passionate engagement from everyone."

A bout a hundred years ago, the great American satirist Mark Twain said, "Always do right. This will gratify some people and astonish the rest." Well, the skepticism that we see about people and their motives is just the root of that quote. It's been around for a long time. And that skepticism flourishes today, fueled by a seemingly nonstop media attention focused on recent business scandals. As the American Enterprise Institute's research shows, business and business leaders in particular, have never enjoyed much prestige in the public eye. Now does that mean that we should simply shrug off this perceived lack of integrity as an inevitability of life? Well, in my view, we definitely should not.

The public's lack of faith in us may not be a new problem, but it's an important problem. We know the antidote for cynicism is obviously not more cynicism. Today businesses of every type grapple with a range of competitive issues, but perhaps the most significant obstacle we must overcome is the skepticism of our customers, employees, shareholders, and the public at large.

They question our motivation and our integrity, our interest in the public good. Simply put, we are not trusted to do the right thing. Abraham Lincoln summed it up best in saying, "Nearly all men can stand adversity, but if you want to put the test of a man's character, give him power." And some business leaders seem to have failed this test. I hasten to add that the perceived lack of integrity is not confined to business.

Today, many of the grandest institutions from government to religion and sports are suffering a crisis of confidence. The absence of faith has led to apathy, to people exercising their right not to participate, and simply opting out of the system. Nowhere is this more evident than in politics. And as an election year, 2004 ought to be a year-long recognition of the duties and privileges that we share as citizens of this country. Instead, many in our country see politics as a ruthless competition among powerful interests, most of which bear little or no resemblance to the public interest. That may or may not be a fair representation of how the system works, but I think it's a fair assessment of how it's perceived. The end product of that perception, not surprisingly, results in apathy.

Some have searched for new solutions, and the notion of values, ethics, and morality have come to the floor. And while better values and standards are always worthwhile, it's important that we clearly delineate the difference between the rules, laws, and ethics of commerce with the laws and principles of God, as we as Latter-day Saints understand them.

In Isaiah 55 we read that God's thoughts are not our thoughts, and that God's ways are not our ways. And Elder Dallin H. Oaks has stated that just as there is a difference between mortals' ways of doing things and the Lord's ways of doing things, so mortals must make significant changes in their ways of doing things when they move from worldly occupations to the performance of Church callings. He also said that some professionals expect that the practices and procedures of the Church will conform to the practices and procedures of professions. Some seek to reconcile the Church and the world by assimilating the doctrines and practices of the Church to the beliefs and practices of the world.

My experience has taught me that while the rules of commerce in our free enterprise, capitalistic system are better than any other economic system the world has seen, and to a great extent are part of the inspired formation of our country, these are still not the same as the laws that govern the kingdom of God. And here are some examples of what I mean.

In business a tried and true rule is the eighty-twenty rule. It states accurately that 20 percent of our efforts will usually yield 80 percent of the benefits. This is generally true regarding customer profitability, product revenues, executive talent, and corporate achievement, because focused effort yields better success than diffused efforts. However, the Lord has his own rule. It's the ninety-nine and one rule that values the contribution and the worth of the individual. His focus is on each and every one.

Another example is the notion of competition, or commercial Darwinism, that suggests that strong corporations and executives survive and excel while weaker institutions fail or go out of business. Rank also means privilege, with the top performers achieving the best there is financially, socially, and receiving the most admiration. The Lord's rule, conversely, is that the strong serve the weak. In fact, the strong are expected to be the servant of all and have an eternal mandate to lift and help those the world may despise.

Again, in business, there are finite resources and wealth that we compete for. With limited supply and resources there is a win-lose rule of work. Act fast, gather wealth, and win. For the Lord, however, there is all that he has, and in his house are many mansions, and there is enough to spare. Winning is not defined by accumulation of resources, since with infinite supply other qualities become paramount.

And lastly, for the world, the intent of the voice or the mind is valued. But for God, the intent of the heart is what matters. Now I think you get the point. But what do we do then to compete and achieve in a world under the established rules of commerce and competition without losing our souls? Well, clearly, we as business and institutional leaders need to set a new tone of the fundamental value of ethics and morality in our organizations. And while participating in the world we must allow our people to rise above the rules of law or commerce as the ultimate measures of our, or their, ethical performance.

The power in a company resides in its leaders: the example they set, what they say, and the way they behave. But, it also resides in the people who go to work every day and are clear about their objectives and are committed to achieving them the right way. Now the real success of a company like Dell doesn't lie solely in our leaders who certify the financial results, but it relies on the people who do the work to make everyday judgment about what's right and what's not. Our goals for our country and our companies will go unfulfilled if we don't demonstrate integrity at every level and earn the trust of our many stakeholders. Customers must trust that we'll deliver what we promise—that our technology is about substance, not about hype, that our products will make their lives simpler and better. Shareholders must trust that the data we share reflects reality and that we are running the business with their interests in mind. And our employees must trust that we're the company with a solid future and that we want their futures to be just as bright as the company's. They need to know that the work they do is important and that their leadership team is acting with integrity and expects them to do the same.

Even the most casual observer is aware of the harm that can befall a company and its people when these trusts are violated. And yet, corporate ethics programs, whose mission ought to be the preservation of that trust, often come across as lip service or window dressing and as something that's tacked on or reactive, rather than something that's integral to the business and to its culture.

Now this is a problem not just for the individual enterprise, but for everybody. Confidence in leading companies like Dell either supports or undermines confidence in the economy and in the market. And confidence, or the lack thereof, can be a self-fulfilling prophecy. Witness the retreat of small investors during the burst of the tech bubble and the subsequent accounting scandals. It's been a hard slog remaining and regaining the trust of those investors. And I believe the trust still remains a fragile one. Those of us in positions of leadership must leave no room for doubt when it comes to the integrity of our financial reporting or business's practices generally.

Now there is the Sarbanes-Oxley Act, which is a motion in our legislative branches designed to acknowledge that something needs to be done to restore the confidence of investors and the public at large. You may debate its merits, and we're doing that today. Some will say it goes too far. Some will say it falls too short. And some will say it's just about right. In my view, that debate, while interesting and useful, may be moot.

At the end of the day, those of us who were clean to begin with will pay a bit more now to prove it. And while not ideal or fair, it's probably an investment we're going to have to make. And those determined to cheat will have to work a bit harder to do so and will suffer the consequences. As for government's role in enforcement, we're all very thankful. But the fact is, you can't legislate ethics. Birds fly, fish are going to swim, and unfortunately, some people are going to cheat. Legislation can't possibly cover every scenario devised by creative cheaters.

So what's the answer? Raising the stakes is certainly part of the answer—shining a brighter light on a company's practices and making it harder and more expensive to do the wrong thing. But speaking as a representative of just one company, the issues that consume me are the ones that I can do something about. I'm referring to how to ensure that our actions at Dell consistently demonstrate ethics and integrity to the people and institutions whose trust we depend on.

It starts with a business model that's transparent to everyone: our customers, our employees, our shareholders, and even our competitors. The Dell direct model is an elegantly simple way of doing business that provides consistent and constant feedback from all of our stakeholders—from the chat-room to the board room. That kind of feedback isn't for the faint of heart. It's the good, it's the bad, and it's the ugly, every single day, every single minute. There's no place to hide, and there's no one else to blame when things go wrong. Our customers and even our employees have other choices in the marketplace and ways to let their voices be heard. Our board of directors has always been an independent and unwavering voice on the behalf of shareholders. The direct model provides the feedback, and our success or failure hinges on how well we listen to that feedback.

The next step is creating a corporate culture of accountability and of responsibility. At Dell, being customer direct means that we are accountable to our customers and to each other every day and at every stage of their experience with our systems. Culture is important because our team is made up of adults whose ethics were often set long before they got to us. What we can do, however, is to establish our expectations and strengthen their resolve as well as their commitment to do the right things. We can appeal to the better aspects of their nature, and if that appeal falls on deaf ears, well, we can recognize that it's time to say goodbye.

As business leaders we spend too much energy focusing on compliance, on meeting our minimal obligations as defined by the law. Our time would be better spent, in my view, developing a fuller picture of who we are, what values define us, and how we can instill those values into the fabric of our organizations and by replacing blame with responsibility. That may sound grandiose, and even a bit idealistic, but at Dell we've been working very hard over the past several years to make what we call "winning with integrity" a very real, very concrete part of who we are. We help our people see and embrace the linkages between our fundamental values, business ethics, and their successes.

Dell turns twenty this year, and for the past couple of years we've devoted a lot time and thought to the transition that we're going through from what you might call adolescence to adulthood. We've done a lot a soul searching about where we've been, who we've become, and what we want to be as we grow up. We're proud of the democratizing effect our direct business model has on the world of technology as we make more technology more affordable for more people around the world. Democratized standards-based innovation, which we're helping to fuel, supports the growth that moves us ever closer to the efficient, effective economy we all want. The more people we're able to empower with technology, the more muscle we can throw behind the ideas and the imagination of our citizens and the better the chance of meeting the challenges in front of us. Realizing our potential as individuals, as a company, and as a society requires passionate engagement from everyone. The passion must also be balanced by maturity, and among other things, maturity means having a clear, explicit, and well-articulated set of beliefs. At Dell we have a set of ideas and principles we want our company to stand for. And we've put those ideas and principles down on paper into something we call "the soul of Dell."

The soul of Dell defines the kind of company we aspire to be. It's a statement to the world that says, this is what we stand for and this is the standard by which we want our actions to be judged. Now we've boiled this soul of Dell down to some fundamental concepts. Things like trust, integrity, honesty, judgment, respect, responsibility, and courage. Most of these speak for themselves, but I'd like to talk a little bit about courage. Because while we cannot create ethical people, as leaders we have a role to play in giving our colleagues the courage it takes to exercise their own ethical responsibilities on behalf of the company and our shareholders. Confucius said it well a long time ago: "To see what is right and not do it is want of courage." How often have all of us come upon a difficult choice of paths, the difficult and possibly righteous path, or the easier and possibly ethically dubious path. In business it's not just your own code of ethics you must factor in, but also that of your organization.

I believe there is a right and a wrong answer and that there is a best answer. But if often takes courage to do the right thing. What we've tried to do at Dell is give our people the courage they need to make the correct choices. We've done this by demonstrating that our ethical commitment is serious and that we collectively agree to what is right first.

Finally, after our transparent business model and a culture of accountability, there have to be processes in place that empower people to do the right thing and to take action when they see something wrong being done. We've established a global ethics council that reports to our board of directors to define and advocate our policies worldwide. It's chaired by our chief ethics officers; I'm a member of that council. Every region throughout our global operations has its own regional ethics committee that reports to that council and places our policies into effect. The council is a true global representation of our business. Our standards for appropriate and ethical behavior are clearly laid out in the Dell code of conduct, including what we call our "higher standard." We train every Dell employee on the elements of the Dell code of conduct. Last year this meant more than forty-four thousand employees in eleven languages, and every new hire gets the training as well.

We also have a global ethics hotline—a whistleblower line, if you will—that provides an anonymous way for employees to report incidents. It is administered by an independent company outside of Dell. Through our twice-yearly Tell Dell Employee Survey, employees have the opportunity to provide confidential feedback on the ethical behavior of their leaders. And those results are reflected in their compensation.

Finally, we have an office that offers employees a comfortable way to resolve work-related issues, including those involving ethics, through a confidential, anonymous, and informal system.

Now all of these processes and initiatives are important, and they give all of our people a way to exercise the courage they need to always do the right thing. Unfortunately, some people are going to cut ethical corners. And for those folks we also have a very simple, easy-to-understand policy regarding their behavior. One strike and you're out. No ambiguity, no equivocation. Ultimately what's lacking in some people is not the courage to do the right thing but the fear of what will happen to them if they do the wrong thing. As leaders of the company, our job is to give them both the carrot and the stick.

I want to emphasize that our commitment goes way beyond just compliance. And, in fact, we hold ourselves to this higher standard, a standard beyond the rule of law. Aleksandr Solzhenitsyn, a Nobel Prize-winning Russian novelist, said in a 1978 Harvard commencement: "I've lived my life in society where there was no rule of law, and that's a terrible existence. But society where the rule of law is the only standard of ethical behavior is equally bad." What that means to me is if we merely aspire to a legal standard of moral excellence, we'll have missed the point. We can and should do better.

A fair question to ask is how this dedication to a higher standard exhibits itself within a very competitive company.

It's important to understand that none of this dulls our competitive edge. We're committed to winning and in fact feel an ethical imperative to compete as hard as we can on behalf of our shareholders, customers, and employees. We idealistically believe that it's a better way to operate and will enhance our ability to win and attract the very best people. The notion of winning with integrity rests on the fact that ethical conduct and winning in the marketplace and in the stock market should and usually do go hand-in-hand, particularly in this era of heightened scrutiny.

Part of the genius of an open free market system is that integrity pays. The way eBay operates is a great example. In this open online bazaar, sellers are ranked by buyers according to how well they deliver what they promised. Sellers with consistently superior scores do much better. So there's an intense pressure to follow through and to live up to your end of the bargain. We need only to look at *Fortune*'s annual rankings of the most admired companies to find examples of companies doing quite well by living up to the higher standard of ethical performance.

Now scandals and corporate malfeasance have been bad for all businesses. But amid the wreckage I believe there's an opportunity for those companies with a track record of ethical principled behavior to differentiate themselves from the pack. In the end, customers, employees, and shareholders gravitate toward companies with stable leadership—those that are credible and have integrity. What Thomas Jefferson called an aristocracy of talent and virtue.

To be sure, numbers that reflect the truth are important. Numbers are the scoreboard, the measuring stick that tells the world how we're doing. We all work in a world of numbers. In fact at Dell, we pride ourselves on being a data-driven, analytic company. But we also recognize that there is an important aspect of leadership that goes beyond the numerically measurable. There is an intangible, inspirational element to our jobs. We need to fight on all fronts in business and politics, everywhere, to erase the cynicism and apathy that undermine both the free market economy and our democracy.

To be worthy of leadership, we must do more than complain about the few bad apples ruining it for the rest of us and seeking someone to blame. We must embrace greater transparency, accountability, for no other reason than it will shine a light on the vast majority of us who are trying to do things the right way. There's plenty of skepticism in the world today, and that in and of itself is not always a bad thing. But my hope is we can balance a healthy skepticism and a reliance on compliance with an increased dose of idealism and responsibility by all stakeholders. Customers, employees, shareholders, citizens, neighbors, voters, everybody, we want something better to believe in. Those of us fortunate enough to be placed in positions of influence have the ability and the duty to give it to them. Emmanuel Conk once said that "morality is not the doctrine of how to be happy but how to be worthy of happiness."

In much the same way, principled, ethical leadership does not guarantee success, although I believe it helps. Rather it ensures that we'll be worthy of success once we've achieved it. And that's my wish for Dell, for myself, for our nation, for all of you. Joseph Smith, when asked how he governed the saints said, "I teach them correct principles and they govern themselves." While not nearly as lofty, our soul of Dell principles seek to teach our people, both leaders and rank-and-file, that there are principles worth fighting for and living for. And that through our adherence to them as people and as a company, we will be more successful and more happy.

KEVIN B. ROLLINS

Kevin Rollins is president and CEO of Dell. Before becoming CEO in July 2004, he served as president and COO, vice chairman, and president of Dell Americas. The company employs approximately 55,200 team members worldwide and reported revenues of $49.2 billion for the past four quarters.

Before joining Dell in April 1996, Rollins was vice president and partner of Bain & Company. While with Bain, he developed strategies around the direct selling of computer systems and services.

Rollins serves at the request of the president of the United States on the Advisory Committee for Trade Policy and Negotiation and is a member of the Computer Systems Policy Project and the U.S. Business Council. He is active in the American Enterprise Institute and the Juvenile Diabetes Research Foundation.

Rollins earned his BA and MBA from BYU and remains an active supporter of the school and university. He is a member of the university's President's Leadership Council and founder of the Marriott School's Rollins Center for eBusiness.

He gave this speech at the Ninth Annual BYU Management Conference 25 June 2004.

THE BUSINESS OF INTEGRITY

by MITT ROMNEY

> *"If you judge your life's success*
> *by the world's standards, you may be elated*
> *or you may be gravely disappointed."*

You cannot imagine how strange it is to be standing here speaking to you, when I remember so distinctly sitting where you are sitting, listening to speakers far more sage than I.

I'm reminded of a family night in our home many years ago. Ann and I sat on the sofa with our boys at our feet. The prescribed story told of a mother who would ask her child to do a certain task. He would reply in case after case, "In a minute, Mommy," and then fail to obey, resulting in predictable calamities like being late for school, losing the puppy, and so forth. When I was finished, my five-year-old, Matthew, asked if he could sit on the sofa and Ann and I sit on the floor; we agreed. Then he said, "Once there was a boy who asked his Mommy for a cookie and she said, "In a minute, Matthew." Turnaround was and is, I guess, fair play.

For some reason, my graduations have stood out quite clearly in my mind. I remember where I sat, by whom, and what I heard. Perhaps that's because of a song we regularly sang at my high school and its graduation. As I sang that song at graduation, I pondered about the future, about time. I wondered what it would be like to look back to this very day: Would I regret my life, would I be satisfied?

The song we sang is the Harrow School song, that of a private boys school in England. A few of its words are:

Forty years on, when afar and asunder
  Parted are those who are singing today,
When you look back and forgetfully wonder
  What you were like in your work and your play—
Then it may be there will often come o'er you
  Glimpses of notes, like the catch of a song;
Visions of boyhood shall float them before you,
  Echoes of dreamland shall bear them along.
Routs and discomfitures, rushes and rallies,
  Bases attempted, and rescued and won.
Strife without anger and art without malice—
  How will it seem to you, forty years on?
God gives us bases to guard or beleaguer,
  Games to play out, whether earnest or fun,
Fights for the fearless, and goals for the eager,
  Twenty, and thirty, and forty years on.

How will it seem to you twenty and thirty and forty years on? What bases will you have chosen to conquer? What games will you have played? Will your life have been a success? To be honest, these questions were very troubling to me as I sat where you are sitting today. Virtually every speaker said something to the effect that life's success was in my control. They quoted authors like Napoleon Hill, who wrote *Think and Grow Rich*, or Anthony Robbins, author of *Unlimited Power*. Success, they said, was up to me—how I prepared and worked, how I thought, how I created and followed a mission statement, or how I put it all together would ensure the success they knew I wanted.

Now, thirty years on, I have come to a very different conclusion. The worldly success stories I have seen result from a blend of factors: yes, the choices you make and control, but also the mental equipment you were born with, more than a fair measure of serendipity, and, where He does choose to intervene, the will of our loving Father. I am not convinced that it's all up to you. Nor do I believe that if you live righteously, your stocks will rise in value, you'll get a promotion, you'll win an election, or you'll get your research published.

I watched my cousin train for the Olympics virtually all his life. He ate right, exercised almost obsessively, competed through college, and placed in national and international competitions. But he got the flu during the Olympic trials and didn't make the U.S. Olympic team—a little unfortunate serendipity at play. I have witnessed the same, time and again, in business, politics, health, entertainment, and education.

I contrast that with the friend I worked with at Bain Capital. She bounced from Bain to Disney in California, then to FTD Florists in Detroit, to Stride Rite Shoes in Boston, and to Hasbro Toys in Providence, Rhode Island. A couple of years ago, a friend called her to ask if she'd help out in his new Internet business. Today, I understand her holdings in eBay have reached almost $1 billion in value. I'm sure that when a success book is written about her life, it will all look so predictable.

There's an element of unpredictability, of uncertainty, of lottery, if you will, in the world that has been created for us. If you judge your life's success by the world's standards, you may be elated or you may be gravely disappointed.

That, of course, is the secret to predictably successful living: the choice of standards by which you will judge your life's success. If by the world's standards, you may well be disappointed, for too many factors for such success are random or out of your control. But there are other standards of success, where chance is not at play.

What will you live for? What bases will you attempt to win?

Some years ago, the firm I founded seemed to be coming apart at the seams. Our five partners were at each other's throats. It seemed we all wanted different things from our lives and from our business. One was consumed with making money; he was obsessed with becoming a member of the Forbes 400. Another wanted power and control. I was of two minds, trying to balance the goals of my faith with the money I was earning. We met with a team-building consultant-psychologist. At the last of our weeklong session, he led us to something transforming.

He said that if we lived our lives in conflict with our core values we would experience stress, ill health, and deep regret. How, we asked, could we know what our core values were? He proceeded to ask us to think of the five or six people we most admired and respected, people currently living or who had ever lived. I chose the Master, Joseph Smith, Abraham Lincoln, and my mother, father, and wife. Then he asked us to write down next to each of those names the five or six attributes we thought of when we thought of that person. The attributes that we had then listed most frequently, he explained, represented our core values. Simply, if we lived in concert with those values, we lived with integrity. We would be happy and fulfilled. And, in contrast, if we lived in a way that was not consistent with those core values, we would ultimately be unfulfilled and unhappy.

To my surprise, all five of my partners revealed the same or similar values: love, family, service, devotion. While we each may have pushed them aside to a different degree in our daily pursuits, they were at each of our centers.

Now, some twenty years later, I have discovered something else about these core values, about living with integrity, about these fundamental measures of successful living: with these at our center, chance does not come into play in determining our success or failure. The ability to live with integrity with the core of our values of love, family, service, and devotion is entirely up to us. Fundamentally, this is the business of successful living.

On my father's eightieth birthday, I asked him what had brought him the most satisfaction in his life, what was his greatest accomplishment. He had been a three-term governor, a United States Cabinet member, presidential candidate, CEO, multimillionaire, and prominent Church leader. His answer was immediate: "My relationship with your mother and with my children and grandchildren is my greatest accomplishment and satisfaction."

Golda Meir, prime minister of Israel, voiced the same truth in an interview on the *Today Show*. She explained that being a mother was her life's greatest accomplishment.

Each lived a life of fulfillment and success, not because of their worldly endeavors, but in spite of them. They lived, rather, in harmony with values unaffected by the vagaries of markets or elections or praise.

If, as you are listening to me today, you are nodding your head in agreement, it's only fair that I warn you that it will not be easy for you to focus your life on achieving your core values. Unfortunately, virtually the entire world around you will ridicule those values and a life based on them—perhaps not overtly, but implicitly in every medium that surrounds you. Some thousands of years ago, the prophet Isaiah looked forward to our times with this observation: "Woe to those who call evil good and good evil, who put darkness for light and light for darkness, who put bitter for sweet and sweet for bitter!"[1]

There is ample evidence of the truth of his observations. In virtually every media, you will see and hear good called evil and evil good, light called dark and dark light. You will hear, for example, that fidelity is boring, that promiscuity is exciting. But if you succumb, you will find why "the love of many shall wax cold."[2]

You will see the malleability of politicians showcased above the unbending character of a Lincoln. In air time and public adulation, vengeance will rise above forgiveness, wealth above charity, power above loyalty, ease above work, luck above preparation. A relentless campaign will be waged for you to substitute the world's values for your values, to cause you to abandon integrity, to subject your measurement of success to uncontrollable chance.

It is empowering, invigorating, and emancipating to live for the success you can control yourself, to live for your most deeply seated values and convictions.

I remember my father's reaction in 1964 when running for governor. President Lyndon B. Johnson had swamped Goldwater, and my dad's pollsters confidently predicted that he'd be pulled under by the Democratic landslide. I was devastated. What would my friends at school think? My dad would be a loser. I looked at him. He looked calm—even relieved. Winning or losing wasn't what was important, he told me. He had done what he felt was right by running in the first place and by speaking out on issues he cared about. The people's votes didn't affect that. He pulled out a familiar quote: "I aspired, and though I achieved not, I was satisfied."

When living in integrity with your core values, your success and fulfillment are not subject to votes, to other's opinions, or to chance.

When John Bennion went to Harvard Business School, he already had a couple of children, one of whom was severely disabled. Then he was called to serve in a Church bishopric.

Because his wife, family, and devotion to God were his core values and measures of success, he accepted the call. He didn't put it off to a time when it would be more convenient, or explain how much work he would have at business school. Surely his grades ended up suffering a little, but his life did not. Now, some twenty-five years on, his family Christmas letter celebrates these same core values, the same life of integrity—a successful life.

You may agree with me now, but unless you purposefully hold fast to living first by your innermost values, you will not succeed. Instead you will enthuse about talks that justify balancing your life, forgetting that "no man can serve two masters." You will read too much into your worldly successes and, perhaps just as dangerously, read too much into your worldly setbacks. They do not measure your worth nor define your success unless you choose for them to do so.

I have watched people of great worldly accomplishments who lived first with integrity for love, family, service, and devotion. In the words of Jacob, "and ye will seek them for the intent to do good."[3]

I have also watched some such people lose their money and their worldly esteem without it eroding their lives, happiness, or their measures of success, for their lives were built on the unshakable foundation of personal integrity, of pursuit of values the world cannot corrupt or disappoint.

Tomorrow, it's a new game for almost all of you. You will choose the bases to be won. Bold, beautiful billboards will beckon you to worldly success. But those bases may unpredictably elude you. Ultimately, even if you attain them, they will not satisfy.

There are other bases to attempt, rescue, and win. These are ones that are in harmony with your most profound values. Achieving them is not a matter of serendipity or chance. With these, your life's success is entirely in your own hands. A decision to live with integrity will make all the difference.

Again, in the words of the Harrow School song:

Forty years on, growing older and older,
  Shorter in wind, as in memory long,
Routs and discomfitures, rushes and rallies,
  Bases attempted, and rescued, and won.
When you look back and forgetfully wonder
  How will it seem to you forty years on?

ENDNOTES
1   Isaiah 5:20.
2   Matthew 24:12.
3   Jacob 2:19.

MITT ROMNEY

Mitt Romney was sworn in as Massachusetts's seventieth governor 2 January 2003. Before being elected to office, Romney was president and CEO of the 2002 Salt Lake Olympic Committee. Under his leadership, the committee erased a $379 million operating deficit, organized more than twenty-three thousand volunteers, and oversaw an unprecedented level of security.

Romney is also founder and former CEO of Bain Capital, Inc., a private holding company with portfolio company revenues in excess of $13 billion. He is a director of Marriott International; Staples, Inc.; The Sports Authority; and LifeLike Corporation. He serves on the national advisory boards of The Points of Light Foundation, The Boy Scouts of America, and City Year.

Romney earned his BA with highest honors from BYU in 1971 and his MBA from Harvard Business School in 1975.

This speech was given at the Marriott School convocation 23 April 1999.

PERFORMANCE WITHOUT PRIDE

by MARK H. WILLES

"We can't look inward and say what can we do;
instead, we must look outward to find what is required,
and then find a way to do it."

This morning I'm going to talk on the subject of "Performance Without Pride." This subject first occurred to me many years ago when, as a member of a stake presidency, I was visiting a small branch in an out-of-the-way part of the state. Those of you who are members of The Church of Jesus Christ know that when a member of the stake presidency comes to visit, especially a small branch, he is usually asked if he would like to speak. Therefore, you can imagine when there were thirty minutes yet to go in the allotted time for the sacrament meeting, and the concluding speaker was saying, "And in conclusion," I started to go through what I would say in my mind. The branch president looked over at me and said, "President, would you like to say something?" Wanting to be appropriately modest, I said, "Well, President, it's up to you." Whereupon, he stood up and closed the meeting.

You can be sure I've worked a little harder on my talks since then. I'm under no illusions as to who I am and what I am, but I have felt impressed, with your permission, to share something that has been very much on my mind, not only those many years ago, but more recently as well.

As I think about you and the world of work or profession to which you will go, the fact is as you receive your diplomas today, you will be congratulated by your family, friends, and faculty. You'll stand tall as you walk across the stage and receive your diplomas. You will go out into the world with a certain degree of confidence—earned confidence—from the work that you have done and the studies you have undertaken. And, you will go into organizations that will expect you to perform; they will expect you to take that knowledge, your abilities, and a certain amount of energy and aggressiveness, and bring to those organizations glory, profits, or some other measure of success. You will be surrounded by people who will always be striving for success and who will be encouraging you to do the same. Therefore, the question and solemn warning is how do we work and stretch for ever-higher levels of performance and success and not fall prey to what President Ezra Taft Benson called the "universal sin?" He said, "Yes, pride is the universal sin, the great vice."

There was a picture in the paper in Minneapolis recently that showed a car sinking into the lake where it had broken through the ice. Right in front of this car was a sign that said "Thin Ice." Underneath the picture was written, "Despite several signs warning lake enthusiasts of 'Thin Ice,' at least three vehicles went through the ice at the public launch site on Spring Park Bay last Tuesday. The same day another vehicle went through the ice on Wayzata Bay and at least six snowmobiles went through thin ice in channel areas around the lake."

Every year warnings of thin ice are given and every year people in cars or snowmobiles go through this ice; tragically, some even die. Like "Thin Ice" signs, I feel strongly that President Benson's statement that "pride is the universal sin" is a warning that we ignore at our peril. Sometimes we seem to acknowledge that we're on thin ice when we say things like "We are humbly proud," as if we could keep the ice from cracking beneath our feet if we just use the right adjective. I doubt that is sufficient. The nice thing is, if we avoid the "sin of pride" we will not only be more righteous, but I strongly believe we will be more effective and more successful in today's competitive and fast-paced world.

To see why this is so, let's look quickly at why President Benson said pride is so bad. Among other things he tells us that:[1]

- Pride is enmity toward our fellowmen. We are tempted daily to elevate ourselves above others and diminish them.
- The proud make every man their adversary by pitting their intellects, opinions, works, wealth, talents, or other worldly measuring device against others.
- It is withholding gratitude and praise that might lift another.

- Selfishness is one of the more common faces of pride. How everything affects me is the center of all that matters—self-conceit, self-pity, worldly self-fulfillment, self-gratification and self-seeking.
- The proud do not receive counsel or correction easily.

There may be some who have these characteristics and are still successful in today's world, but I believe strongly there really is a better way. All of the characteristics that President Benson listed come from people who are focused inward on themselves. There is a growing body of evidence that demonstrates that to be successful in today's world, we must focus outward not inward. For example, many businesses used to design and manufacture a product or a service, add on a margin, and then sell it to their customers—take it or leave it. In today's world where everyone is cost-conscious, you have to start with what someone is willing to pay for a product or service, and then work backward to figure out how to make it or provide it at that price and still earn an adequate profit. We can't look inward and say what can we do; instead, we must look outward to find what is required, and then find a way to do it.

Similarly, many businesses have assumed that they "knew" what their customers needed in terms of product or service attributes, only to watch in dismay as other companies came along—less prideful and more outwardly focused—who asked their customers what they wanted and then designed products or services accordingly, and promptly won the business for themselves. Even governments at the local, state, and national level are finding that their customers, the citizens, are fed up with the lack of responsiveness to their individual needs. People want governmental pride, arrogance, and paternalism replaced with effectiveness and responsiveness, or they would just as soon see government get out of those activities. Consequently, organizations of all kinds must increasingly be externally focused on customers and consumers. Since organizations are made up of individuals, the more externally focused those individuals are, the more successful their organizations will be.

It is difficult for us to compartmentalize our lives. If we are selfish and self-centered, we are less likely to be externally-focused and effective. And yet it is precisely that kind of external focus and sensitivity that is, and increasingly will be, the hallmark of successful organizations.

Moving down to the individual level, there is another element at work that is also critical to our success. People who are prideful, self-centered, and try to get ahead at the expense of others, soon come to be distrusted by those around them. Yet the world is moving in directions where greater trust is required. In plants, team-based, high-performance work systems are replacing more traditional forms of manufacturing. In marketing and service companies, teams of marketing, finance, R&D, manufacturing, and other specialists are being formed to coordinate resources, and better meet the needs of customers. When designing new products or services, teams from marketing, finance, research, engineering, and manufacturing are pulled together to drastically cut the time and expense involved in development. In the same spirit, teams of companies called alliances are increasingly being formed to share expertise and increase mutual opportunities for success. For example, companies are forming alliances with their suppliers to reduce costs, improve quality, and increase speed and innovation. In addition, companies are forming strategic alliances to be able to do together what neither could do as well alone. General Mills has formed three international joint ventures in the last five years that by the year 2000 will have sales of well over $3 billion.

To work effectively and successfully in what is increasingly a team- or alliance-based environment, we must be trusted. It is hard to trust someone who is always thinking of himself or herself first. It is much easier to trust someone who is focused outward and sensitive to the needs of others. Consequently, pride is not only unattractive, but it will increasingly get in the way of personal effectiveness and success. By their very nature, teams and alliances require sharing, giving, helping, trusting—the very opposite of the selfishness of pride.

One of the reasons I feel so strongly about this subject is that often in my life when I have made my biggest mistakes, I did so because of pride. In some cases, I thought I knew the answers, when in fact I didn't, and I didn't seek for or listen to enough different points of view to adjust my own thinking fast enough. In other cases, as President Benson said, I did not receive counsel or correction easily. I allowed pride to reinforce my own natural stubbornness. I would dismiss criticism when in fact the criticism was valid. Consequently, it took me longer to adjust my actions or my behavior. When speed is so important in today's world, we can't take too long to get it right. If we take too long to get it right, it's not right because the opportunity has already passed us by.

Let me tell you one quick story—a story that I'm embarrassed to tell you because it happened while I was preparing this talk. My wife and I were sitting at a table with the head of a large manufacturing organization, and I decided to boast. General Mills had just done something that I thought was really quite interesting. We make a large range of food products. We make a number of those same products on the same line in our plants— they are multifaceted plants. When we change from one product to another, one package size to another, it can take us anywhere from three to five hours to stop the equipment, clean the equipment, change the dials to put the new additions on, and then start it up again. Our people said to themselves, "We need to find a way to go from three to five hours to ten minutes. We've got to do it faster." If you multiply the changeover times by the number of times we do it in all of our plants, the cost is horrendous. So they decided they'd go out to the pit stops at NASCAR racing tracks and watch the cars come racing in—the wheels come off, the gas goes in, the wheels go back on and the cars all get out of the pit stop in about thirty seconds. They took videotapes of what was going on, took it back to the plant, took the principles that they learned from the pit stop, and applied it to the changeover on this line. Sure enough, they went from three hours to seventeen minutes, and they'll have it down to ten minutes next month.

I was impressed; I was excited; I thought I'd brag about it to my associate from this other manufacturing company. He listened with kind of a smile on his face and he said, "That's wonderful, that's terrific." I said, "Well, how do you do it?" He said, "Well, we were in much worse shape than you. It used to take us sometimes seventeen hours to make a changeover on our line. We did exactly the same thing you did—we went to the Indianapolis Speedway, went to the pit stop, and we now have the changeover down to ten minutes on every line in every plant in our system." I'm bragging about one line in one plant and he has it in every line in every plant in the system. I was embarrassed. I should have been embarrassed. And then I learned a great lesson. I went back to our people and said, "Ah, you think you're good; let me tell you what I've just learned." Their response was fascinating. When they heard that somebody was way ahead of them, they said, "Great. Can we go learn from them?" I wanted to brag; they wanted to learn. That is the difference.

So what do I suggest to you as you graduate? Choose worthy, honorable work. Set high standards of performance and beat them. Get that performance by focusing on and being sensitive to the needs of others—consumers, customers, and co-workers. And remember that, even with your great BYU education, you don't know it all. Listen to corrective suggestions and counsel. Seek ideas and evaluations from others. Be teachable—responsive to the things that you learn. And stay away from the thin ice of pride. Going through the ice into the water is no fun. I know; I live in Minnesota where the wind chill is minus eighty degrees. Thank you very much. Good luck and God bless you.

ENDNOTE

1   Benson, Ezra Taft. (1989, May). "Beware of pride." *Ensign*, 19. pp. 4–7.

MARK H. WILLES

Mark Willes is former CEO *and publisher of* Times Mirror Co.*, a consumer and professional information company that published the* Los Angeles Times *and* Baltimore Sun*. Before joining* Times Mirror*, Willes was vice chairman of General Mills and a former senior official with the Federal Reserve.*

He recently completed three years as president of the Hawaii Honolulu Mission of The Church of Jesus Christ of Latter-day Saints. He is a distinguished professor of management at the Marriott School and recipient of BYU's *1995 Jesse Knight Industrial Citizenship Award.*

He received his AB *degree in 1963 from Columbia College in New York City, and his PhD in 1967 from Columbia Graduate School of Business.*

This address was given at the BYU *Marriott School convocation 28 April 1995.*

INTEGRITY OF THE ASCENT

by GARY P. WILLIAMS

*"Don't sacrifice what you want most in your career
for what you want at the moment."*

T hroughout our lives we may ascend to many summits.
These climbs have unique challenges that require us to
prepare and approach each one differently. Some of
these climbs may be approached in a reckless and nonchalant
manner with little concern for the final outcome, while others
require careful planning and route consideration.

Your career is one of the most important summits you will
ascend—one that requires much planning and attention to the
route that you will travel. The ultimate goal may require a combination of years of education, followed by on-the-job training,
certifications, tutoring, mentoring, and learning through trial and
error. Once we reach the final approach to the summit, we may
walk the distance alone or lead those who have followed us.

I believe the integrity of the ascent is paramount to our ultimate success. The four principles that must be present if we are to reach the summit with integrity are: planning, preparation, listening, and obedience.

PRINCIPLE I: PLAN ~ *Develop and commit to worthy lifetime goals.* My family enjoys summiting mountains. We've climbed most of the peaks in this part of the country–Timpanogos, Nebo, Pfeifferrhorn, Olympus, Deseret, and others and have traveled as far as California to climb Mt. Shasta and Mt. Whitney (the highest peak in the continental United States). In August 2000, we decided to undertake a lifetime goal to summit Mt. Kilimanjaro in Tanzania, Africa. I would like to compare what we learned on our climb to what I have learned as I have ascended my career path.

Mt. Kilimanjaro ranks as the tallest peak on the African continent at 19,340 feet—the highest freestanding mountain in the world. The ascent allows the climber to travel through several climatic zones, beginning in a tropical forest, traveling through the alpine desert, and ending at an altitude where almost nothing can survive. Our climbing team consisted of local guides, support personnel, and twelve American climbers including three of my children: Amanda, age seventeen; Heidi, age twenty-two; and Philip, age fifteen.

Our earliest preparations included a review of optional routes and trip plans. Some options offered a "quick" four-day climb—less camping, exposure, and discomfort. At the other end of the spectrum was a nine-day climb—seven nights on the ascent with the eighth on the return. It required more hiking, camping, cold nights, exposure, and cost. But, it offered something else, a 90 percent success rate for reaching the summit compared with less than 50 percent success on the other routes. The risk of contracting altitude sickness is a real and potentially dangerous condition that can be mitigated if a climber is willing to spend more time at various elevations en route to the summit.

Though it would require more sacrifice than the shorter, more often used climbs, the Shira Plateau route rewards the patient climber with a greater chance of reaching the summit. We determined to follow the advice of President David O. McKay: "The greatest mistake we make in this life is giving up what we want most for what we want right now."

When I was sixteen, a wise man taught me an important concept. An advisor to my youth group, invited any of us who were interested to develop a ten-year plan with his help and to visit him at his work. I took him up on both offers.

My advisor was a skilled and well-known engineer. He was involved in the design of the first microwave oven and had received much acclaim for his work. While visiting his office, I discovered he had resigned his position as the engineering manager to make a lateral move into another department. As the manager of this department, he received no pay increase and kept the same title.

When I asked him why he made such a move, he responded that what he really wanted in his career was to "run the company." By traveling the longer, more difficult path he felt he had a better chance of achieving what he wanted most, the top position in the firm.

That day changed my life. I too wanted to "run a company." I set about educating myself and developing skills in two functional areas: finance and marketing. My decision was to travel a longer path.

After college I accepted a position as a financial analyst with a large U.S. corporation. When the opportunity presented itself, I transferred into the strategic planning group. At first, my associates' careers seemed to be developing more quickly as they rose in the financial group where I started my career. But it was not long before I was given the director of strategic planning position for my corporate division and soon thereafter was promoted to marketing manager within the group. What I wanted most was now in my sights as I began to acquire the skills that I would eventually need in my career pursuits.

Don't sacrifice what you want most in your career for what you want at the moment. If your career summit trek requires more distance and a more costly path, don't be afraid to accept the challenge.

PRINCIPLE 2: PREPARE ~ *Get an education, learn the skills of your trade, and then execute your plan with vigor.*
We remained two nights at camp four on Mt. Kilimanjaro, located approximately 15,000 feet above sea level. There, we learned the skills of high-altitude trekking—how to place one foot in front of the other and pausing before taking the next step. We climbed more than one thousand feet, practicing our skills

before descending to our camp that evening. I must admit I was not convinced that our efforts would be rewarded, but our guide insisted we needed to learn the skill if we were to succeed.

Let me relate this principle to a business experience. In 1998, our business decided to hire an investment banker to help find a potential buyer or partner for our company. By the fall of that year, we were deep into discussions with an NYSE listed company regarding the potential acquisition of the company. During the next few months, I called upon every skill I had acquired during my education and trek through corporate life. As we reviewed our statements of past performance and developed complicated financial proformas requested by the acquiring company, I reflected back to the "pain" that I endured in William Edwards' finance class during my BYU undergraduate program.

Dr. Edwards was a successful business and academic professional who believed in steep ascents—no easy walks through his class. He firmly believed in the old adage, "No pain, no gain." My day at fifteen thousand feet learning the right-stride technique was much like the many hours spent working on projects in his finance class. Though my desire may have been to avoid the effort, I was willing to endure the pain for the education. He required excellence in everything we did. By the way, we successfully sold the company—I wish that Dr. Edwards were still with us so I could thank him personally.

Consider the following points during your educational experience here at BYU.

- Get a good education, not just a degree.

- Seek opportunities for applied experiences—such opportunities exist in field studies classes and in classes that offer an opportunity to work with businesses.
- Find jobs and internships that support your academic program.
- Take risks in the classroom and in business situations—raise your hand in class, participate in discussions.
- Be involved in extracurricular activities—join clubs, participate in competitions such as the Business Plan Competition.

PRINCIPLE 3: LISTEN ~ *Seek counsel from those you trust.*

As we consider seeking counsel, it's worth remembering what Norman Vincent Peale said, "The trouble with most of us is that we would rather be ruined by praise than saved by criticism."

Day one of the Kilimanjaro climb was a 1,500-foot ascent over approximately five miles in a tropical forest. Monkeys, elephants, and tropical birds populated this area of lush vegetation. Because of the humidity, I wore a pair of waterproof boots instead of my more comfortable mountain-climbing boots that I had packed away for later in the climb. The boots were broken in and had carried me up many mountains. By the time that we had reached the lunch stop, I began to develop blisters and hoped that two pairs of socks would solve my problems. I spent most of the rest stop administering to my poor feet.

I arrived at camp that evening with severe blisters and still had several days of climbing ahead of me. Words cannot describe the great anxiety I felt. We gathered together as a family in a small tent, and I told my children of my condition. I honestly didn't know if I could continue. We had worked so hard to reach this point, and now all seemed lost. We shed some collective tears and decided to wait until morning before making a final decision.

That night, my mind raced as I worried about what to do. Should I descend from the mountain, leaving my children with people I barely knew to continue the ascent? Or, should I continue on, risking even more injury to my feet and perhaps a more difficult evacuation from the mountain? At daylight, I approached our guide, Alex, to discuss my alternatives.

I left my tent and walked over to where Alex was camped. He opened his tent flap, and I explained to him the situation. He listened carefully and then began to counsel me on what he felt was best. "Gary, we need to take this one day at a time," he said. "We can't solve all of the 'what ifs', but we can deal with this each day and do what is needed to keep you on the climb." Alex then concluded, "As we face what appear to be overwhelming obstacles, we hinder our ability to move forward by overprocessing information."

I agreed with his plan and prepared to leave camp with my family. I covered my feet in moleskin (a hiker's best friend when blisters develop), leaving holes in the spots where I had developed blisters. I switched boots and moved on to camp two. Each day Alex and I discussed the situation, and my children helped administer to my needs.

John Wooden, perhaps the greatest coach in the history of college basketball, once said, "It's what we learn after we think we know it all that really counts." Alex taught me what was needed to continue the quest.

In my career I often struggled with how I could move from the life of a corporate executive to that of an entrepreneur. I had learned how to run a business, but I lacked the idea to start something new. My church responsibilities allowed me to become good friends with a local leader. Over the years, I gained confidence in his ability to mentor me on professional decisions.

He had a very successful business developing large tracts of land and building homes. Much like me, he knew how to run a business but lacked the skills needed in his industry. He partnered with someone who was skilled in the construction trades, and together they built one of the largest businesses in their market.

As we talked I recognized my skills were similar to his talents. He helped give me the vision that would eventually lead me to form a partnership with a skilled professional in software development. Together, my partner and I were able to take a company that we bought and build it into the largest firm of its size in our market.

As we read in Proverbs 13:20, "He that walketh with wise men shall be wise: but a companion of fools shall be destroyed." Over the years I have chosen carefully those who I considered mentors. These lifetime guides have provided for me insight, inspiration, confidence, consolation, and often just a listening ear.

PRINCIPLE 4: OBEY ~ *Be true to yourself and to your conscience.*
There were several times on the mountain when we turned to that inner voice of reason and guidance. The daily routine

revolved around arising early, eating, breaking camp, traveling to a lunch stop, trekking on to the day's destination, and setting up camp. The porters assumed the backbreaking work by carrying all the essential food and supplies, including our gear. We carried only those items needed during the day.

The division of labor troubled my children; their consciences would not permit them to watch as others labored. Each morning, they would help with the camp duties. To be true to what they believed, they knew that they must help, even though they were tired. At the Crater Camp at 18,500 feet it was difficult to breathe and extremely cold. Liquids would freeze in a matter of seconds and the basics of life, eating and sleeping, were uncomfortable. The kids labored on. They never compromised their values. I love them for what they did and how they behaved. They didn't need to help, to assist those whose responsibility it was to labor in the camp, but they did anyway. The affection of the porters and the friends that they made through their actions are remembered to this day.

One of the greatest examples of being true to ourselves and acting as we know we should is the life of George Washington. After leading the country through the struggle of the Revolutionary War, Washington could have become the first king of America. Many wanted him to assume the role. Instead he shied away from leadership and needed to be convinced to return to the service of his country. In her book, *The Miracle at Philadelphia*, Catherine Drinker Bowen finds that "Washington's genius lay in his character."

While living on the West Coast I had the opportunity to work with a fast-growing technology and manufacturing firm. I negotiated a stock option to purchase an ownership position in the firm after two years of employment. Three individuals founded the company and had never allowed anyone to buy into the firm.

The terms of my buy-in were very favorable and would guarantee my future with the company. One or two of the owners would be retiring within a short period of time, and I was set to move into a position of significant responsibility. As I considered my actions, all logic pointed to my exercising the ownership option and securing my position.

As I explored my inner feelings, I knew what was right for me and my family. If I were to be true to myself, I would need to decline the option to purchase stock, which would signal to the founders that I was not going to stay with the firm. I knew that my value system differed from theirs and that I would possibly never be comfortable as their partner. As I look back on that decision, it was the right one in every way. What seemed to be too good to be true was just that.

Staying with that firm may have precluded the other opportunities in my life for which I am grateful. We can learn much from what we know to be right; we must develop the courage to act on the promptings of our conscience.

What is the result of following the four principles of planning, preparation, listening, and obedience as we ascend the summits of our lives? In the case of our attempt to climb Mt. Kilimanjaro, it meant reaching the summit on 13 August 2000.

As you consider your career path, let me share with you an anonymous quote that I carry with me in my planner. "Our achievements are shaped by the terrain of our lives and the strength of the foundations we set. In building the life we've imagined, we must be true to our beliefs, dare to be ethical, and strive to be honorable. For integrity is the highest ground to which we can aspire."

If we are willing to strive with integrity in our lives, I believe that we will not only succeed in our ascents, but we will also cast a light on others and the organizations that we serve. Let me conclude with a quote from the movie *Anna and the King*. Anna is preparing to depart Siam. The boy King Chulalongkom is looking at Anna and begins to reflect on the influence that she has had on the people and country of Siam.

"It is always surprising how small a part of life is taken up by meaningful moments; most of them are over before they start, although they cast a light on the future and make the person who originated them unforgettable." Anna had shined such a light on Siam.

I wish the best for you as you cast your own light on the future and achieve success in your careers through integrity in planning, preparing, listening, and obeying.

GARY WILLIAMS

Gary Williams is past president and CEO *of Sterling Wentworth Corporation/SunGard Expert Solutions—a market leader in the* design, development, and marketing of smart-technology solutions for the financial services industry.

Williams is associate director of BYU's Center for Entrepreneurship and a teaching professor at the Marriott School. A member of the Utah Angels, Williams is involved in investing in new ventures. He serves on the advisory boards of several corporations.

Williams earned his BS from BYU in 1973 and his MBA from Arizona State University in 1974.

He gave this address to students when he was recognized as the 2003 Marriott School Honored Alum 9 October 2003.

INDEX

COLOPHON

Typeset in Fournier and Geometric 415, Bitstream's version of Metro. Printed by Brigham Young University Press on Color Source cream 70 lb. text. Bound by Evermind Productions in Holliston Arrestox navy vellum. Endsheet is Rainbow antique delft 80 lb. text vellum.